THE
RETIRING
MIND

How to Make the Psychological
Transition to Retirement

Robert P. Delamontagne, PhD

Synergy Books

646.79
D336

The Retiring Mind: How to Make the Psychological Transition to Retirement
Published by Synergy Books
P.O. Box 80107
Austin, Texas 78758

For more information about our books, please write us, e-mail us at info@
synergybooks.net, or visit our web site at www.synergybooks.net.

Printed and bound in China. All rights reserved. No part of this book may be reproduced in any form or by any electronic or mechanical means including information storage and retrieval systems without permission in writing from the copyright holder, except by a reviewer, who may quote brief passages in review.

Publisher's Cataloging-in-Publication
(Provided by Quality Books, Inc.)

Delamontagne, Robert P.
  The retiring mind : how to make the psychological
  transition to retirement / by Robert P. Delamontagne.
    p. cm.
  Includes bibliographical references.
  LCCN 2009934044
  ISBN-13: 978-0-9823140-9-8
  ISBN-10: 0-9823140-9-4

  1. Retirement--Psychological aspects. 2. Retirement
--Planning. 3. Retirees--Psychology. 4. Personality
and situation.   I. Title.

HQ1062.D43 2010   646.7'9
                    QBI09-600131

10 9 8 7 6 5 4 3 2 1

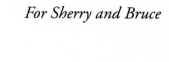
For Sherry and Bruce

Contents

Acknowledgments

Knowledge is dynamic and spirited while it relentlessly accelerates and grows. It is initiated at some faraway place and time, by an obscure source, and then seems to assume a new identity—riding an indecipherable wave to unknown ports. I am certainly fortunate to know precisely where the intellectual foundation for this book originated and am deeply indebted to the following:

- Claudio Naranjo, MD, for providing deep knowledge of the Enneagram typologies portrayed in his book *Character and Neurosis: An Integrative View*.

- A. H. Almaas (Hameed Ali) for his introduction and description of Holy Ideas and how they relate to each Enneagram type as described in his book *Facets of Unity: The Enneagram of Holy Ideas*.

- David Hawkins, MD, PhD, for completely altering my understanding of human consciousness through his book *Power vs. Force: The Hidden Determinants of Human Behavior.*

Preface

The quality and texture of our lives are greatly determined by the challenges that occupy our minds and confiscate our thinking. I have learned this through many years of experience as an entrepreneur and educational psychologist. For whatever reason, my life has largely focused on trying to understand why people are the way they are (including myself). How does the mind work? How does learning occur? What is the most effective way to teach? At the time of my retirement, I felt that I was well prepared for the transition. I had financial security, good health, a loving family, and hopes for the future. What I actually experienced when I retired were fleeting moments of happiness, much longer periods of boredom, and feelings of aimlessness. It got worse over time until I realized I was living in a self-imposed "dead zone" where my usual zest for life was nowhere to be found. Was my chronic malaise unique only to me? After reviewing the research and talking with many friends and family members who have recently retired, I have come to the conclusion that this problem is much more widespread than commonly thought.

Most of the articles and books I have read about retirement seem to indicate that if you have enough money to meet your daily living expenses, retirement is a cinch. They also suggest that retiring will be more fulfilling if you sell your house and move to the Sunbelt, where the soft southern breezes blow your troubles away. In the midst of this "don't worry, be happy" mantra, there is seldom any mention that retirement often causes major emotional upheavals on the same scale as the death of a loved one, loss of a job, or a financial crisis caused by a bad investment. I have come to learn that this emotional distress is often subtle in nature. It doesn't announce itself with fanfare, but sneaks up and taps you on the shoulder. One day, you get out of bed, start your day, and realize you are not happy. You don't feel like yourself, and the activities you planned for the day do not bring you pleasure. You feel like you have lost power over your own life. You don't know what it is that will make you happy. You left one life behind but don't have a new life to live. You know what you don't want to do, but not what you want to pursue instead. Uncomfortable feelings of confusion and helplessness often result.

Unfortunately, this unhappiness does not restrict itself to you, but spreads to those around you. Your immediate family and close friends notice that you are not your usual upbeat self. You may be excessively controlling or hypercritical, followed by surprising outbursts of anger. As a friend recently said in jest, "I used to love my husband until he retired." Your social life may decline because you no longer feel like going out. You could spend long periods alone in introspection and contemplation searching for answers to your dilemma. You may engage in antisocial behavior, having marathons in front of the TV or self-medicating through alcohol or drug abuse. Worse yet, in an attempt to alleviate your distress, you may make a major life-changing decision, such as selling your house or moving to a different state, only to learn that this creates even more anxiety.

I realize that many retirees may never encounter these problems. According to research studies, these fortunate individuals most likely have looked forward to retirement for a long time, have sufficient savings, are in good health, have pensions or IRAs to maintain their needs, have many friends popping in unannounced, and have active social lives. They make friends easily and regularly go to church or other structured group activities such as sporting events, reading clubs, or political rallies. They have hobbies such as woodworking, bridge, car repair, golf, gardening, photography, or computer programming that bring them great pleasure. It is noteworthy that those of us suffering in the retirement doldrums don't want to be like these people; indeed, it creates an interesting problem. We want to find happiness in retirement on our own terms and are not willing to change our identities in the process. You should be happy to know this is entirely possible and this book goes into depth on the subject.

My quest for understanding and resolving my own psychological adjustment to retirement led me to write *The Retiring Mind*. I wanted to free myself from the mental angst I had been experiencing and better manage my new life. At the same time, I also wanted to help others who were planning for retirement or experiencing the same emotions and frustrations that were sapping my energy. Along the way, I learned a great deal about the causes of my adjustment problem. I learned that successfully navigating the rocky shoals leading to a happy retirement required a deeper comprehension of the idiosyncrasies of my personality and the adoption of a new set of spiritual principles. I came to realize that both my personal style and spiritual beliefs were simply two sides of the same coin upon which my happiness in retirement depended. Now I grasp what Tolstoy meant when he said, "Truth, like gold, is to be obtained not by its growth, but by washing away from it all that is not gold." When I washed away everything that was not my personal truth, I discovered my gold. I believe that the lessons I learned can help you uncover your own gold during your transition into retirement.

You are not alone in this quest. As you will soon discover, you are an active participant in one of the greatest social transformations of all time. During a recent interview, Social Security Commissioner Michael J. Astrue told The Associated Press that more than eighty million baby boomers are expected to be added to the social security system at an estimated rate of ten thousand per day for the next twenty years.[1]

If you don't take the positive action necessary to better manage your transition into retirement, you are just burning precious daylight. The truth is that you don't have unlimited time available. Your most important responsibility after liberating yourself from the daily grind is to experience happiness and fulfillment, not distress and emotional turmoil. If you agree and want to squeeze all of the juice out of your remaining years, hopefully the content of this book will guide your way as it did mine.

I recall Dr. David Hawkins, the distinguished author and lecturer, stating, "It's not easy being a human being." We don't live in heaven, and nirvana is not easily accessible. Being a productive and effective person often takes great effort. To make progress, you have to be willing to do the work. Thomas Mann once wrote, "Introspection is the first step toward transformation, and I understand that, after knowing himself, nobody can continue being the same." As you read this book I ask you to be introspective, and contemplate any personal insights you may gain from these pages. Enjoy the process of learning about yourself and try to feel the truth as it reveals itself to you.

---

1. Associated Press, "Social Security Unveils New Online Application: Agency Braces for Wave of 10,000 Boomers a Day Applying for Benefits," MSNBC, January 6, 2009, http://www.msnbc.msn.com/id/28528198.

Chapter 1

Is That All There Is?

When I retired at age sixty-three, I calculated that I had about seventeen years left to live. I simply subtracted my age from the average life expectancy of an adult male, which is approximately eighty years. I knew that I had a better chance of living longer since both of my parents lived into their nineties; however, I also knew there are no sure things in life and that I would be lucky to live seventeen more years. I had never really thought seriously about my own mortality. I believe I subconsciously felt as though I would live forever. To actually put a time limit on my life was sobering. What did I want to do? How did I want to live? What things were most important to me? How long would I be in good health? Had I met the requirements for eternity, whatever they may be? For the first time in my life, I had no answers. I had fallen into a black hole where there were no guideposts for me to follow.

What had happened to me? I built a successful company and lived a very active and dynamic life. I traveled the world, was financially successful, met talented and interesting people, and had no serious health problems; overall I had a great life. Yet I had no clue what to do next. For the first time in twenty-five years, I did not have a company to manage, nothing that urgently needed to be done, and, most troubling, no one who needed me to make a decision or contribute to a discussion. I did not play golf, nor belong to any clubs, and had little interest in doing either. I wish that I had though, because brother, was I screwed.

To deal with this dilemma, I began looking outside of myself for the answers. I began looking for diversions. I almost bought a house at the beach, only to back out at the last minute. I am truly thankful to this day for a small thread of assistance from the Man Upstairs because I could easily be the proud owner of a large beach house in an area that I did not like, at a price I could not afford. All I needed was a little danger to keep it interesting. How about a boat, a motorcycle, or better yet, a Porsche? That would do it. I could already feel the wind in my hair and the sun in my face. Again, I was blessed. I did not buy the boat or motorcycle, but in a moment of weakness, I did purchase a late-model Porsche. I have to admit that it is fun to drive, but it didn't even come close to solving my problem. I learned that adding things to your life often creates a heavy burden. They are expensive to acquire, require constant maintenance, usually decline in value, and, in the end, almost never provide the pleasure you expected.

Well if the answer was not outside of myself, I guess that meant I had to look inside. I don't know about you, but I would rather do almost anything that's legal than spend much time thinking about myself. Frankly, I don't find myself all that interesting. I knew deep down that the path to my happiness during the time I had left was somewhere deep inside of me. I knew I had to unwind myself layer by layer until I gained the insights I needed to move forward with confidence. This book is about the adventure I took and what I learned—how I found relative peace in retirement—and will hopefully be a beacon of hope to those who follow.

Achievement Addiction

Most high achievers I know have encountered emotional difficulties in retirement because they miss the action of their professional life and can't seem to live without it. Whether they work in an office building, a hospital, or a factory, high achievers have several traits in common. They are focused, disciplined individuals who are highly respected by their superiors and coworkers because they are good at what they do. Their self-image largely stems from their identity as diligent, smart, and very capable individuals who have earned the respect of their customers and work associates. Seldom are these people physically or mentally idle; they think about work all the time. These achievers are extremely focused, dedicated, and hardworking, which are fundamental requirements for high performance.

There are two main components essential for success: knowing more than others and exerting more effort for achievement. Unfortunately, both of these characteristics, over time, limit the opportunities for cultivating interests outside of the workplace and make high achievers less diversified in their interests.

You may be wondering what motivates these individuals to make such extreme commitments of time and energy to achievement. The answer is that even though work can be highly stressful at times, these high achievers find it interesting and enjoyable. They take pleasure in the challenge of competition and problem solving. Their payoff is high self-esteem, intellectual stimulation, pride, respect, and financial rewards. In most instances, they receive a great deal of recognition and satisfaction from their work. In fact, there is no other place where the opportunities exist for such a high return from one's abilities and accomplishments, which is why high achievement is addictive. As with all addictions, there is a price to pay, even though some may consider this to be a positive addiction.

I am an expert on achievement addiction because I suffered from it. I started a business in the basement of my home in 1980 that became one of the first computer-based training companies in the U.S. I didn't know it at the time, but I helped invent the technology-based education industry, now called online learning. The company I founded, EduNeering, Inc., evolved through the years and was sold in 2007 to Kaplan, Inc. The company is now called Kaplan EduNeering and is based in Princeton, New Jersey.

Over the years, I subtly became addicted to my business. It occupied over 90 percent of my waking hours for twenty-five years. It was extremely interesting and challenging to me. I enjoyed my relationships with customers and the camaraderie and teamwork involved in running a successful business. Where else can this be found after retirement? The answer is nowhere.

It is simply not possible to recreate the same opportunities for mental stimulation that exist in the workplace. We have all seen well-known and highly accomplished athletes and executives who seem unable to relinquish their old lives. Many of them suffer intense pain related to divorce or alcohol and drug abuse, and often end up making serious investment mistakes. This all occurs in a desperate attempt to get their old groove back. In essence, they want to quell the pain, find their lost mojo, and regain feelings of accomplishment.

Many high achievers feel as though their self-worth is diminished if they are not accomplishing something important. Their life becomes a marathon of accomplishments, based on the notion that it is personally threatening to be idle for any length of time. I can recall going to the beach on vacation and taking my bike so I could exercise while my wife spent time relaxing in the sand and surf. I would explore the beach towns and the local neighborhood haunts. Occasionally I would stop and talk to fisherman and learn more about the area, but usually I would just rack up the miles. I have never spent more than ten minutes on the beach in my life—pathetic I know.

Another driving force behind achievement addiction is fear of failure. You see, failure is unthinkable for high achievers. They will do almost anything to succeed. If that means working twenty-four hours a day, so be it. If it means exposing themselves to danger, let's get it on. I can remember driving sixty miles to a client meeting during a blizzard when all the schools and government agencies were closed. I spun out a few times but arrived on time. The only person in the entire office at that early hour was the CEO. I could sense that he was slightly uncomfortable because none of his top executives made it into the office that morning, whereas I had driven sixty miles in a blinding snowstorm for the meeting. Fear of failure motivated me to do whatever it took to succeed. At the time I thought nothing of it, but now that I think about it, I took an unnecessary risk. The key point is that accomplishment makes achievers feel safe; lack of accomplishment makes them feel personally vulnerable because their self-worth, the financial security of their employees, and the success of their business all depend upon their high achievement.

As I write this book, we are experiencing the worst recession of my lifetime. Think about how we got into this situation—who exhibited the risky behavior that resulted in this financial disaster? You guessed it— achievement addicts. I can only imagine the extent of the psychological pain that exists among these driven individuals who feel there is little or nothing they can do to repair the economic catastrophe they caused, not to mention the pain felt by those high achievers who lost a large percentage of their hard-earned savings and investments. I recall receiving e-mails from my investment bankers that were written at eleven o'clock at night while they were still in the office. *What's a little sacrifice when there is so much work to do?* they thought. Unfortunately, I would agree with them.

In the achievement addict's profile is the notion of living large—living life on a grand scale. This is very appealing because it is an outward sign of success. It is also a sign of autonomy and independence from restrictions. Leading a life of sovereignty is character-ized by great freedom of action. From the perspective of family and friends, highly successful people appear to defy gravity by living lives that seem to have no boundaries. Inside of their organizations, they are granted special dispensation thanks to their well-known reputations for getting results. Are you going to look over the shoulder of an investment banker who has racked up large financial gains year in and year out? How about the middle manager who has had outstanding performance appraisals several years in a row? Everyone in an organization knows who the high performers are who receive special rec-ognition and attention. These people need gratitude and acknowledgement to feel good about themselves. If they don't receive sufficient positive feedback, they go into withdrawal and feel dissatisfaction, or take their talents elsewhere. Deep inside, they know the price they are paying to maintain their performance level, and they expect appropriate recognition.

You can imagine what happens when these achiev-ers retire and move into an environment where little or no positive feedback occurs—where high performance is not required. It is like having an individual whose motor is running at 8,000 rpms in an environment where idle speed is all that is required. How do they back off their speed when it is a part of the personality that has served them well for thirty years? I recently met a seventy-five-year-old gentleman who was a retired CEO of a major company. We were in a group setting having a few drinks. As I watched him move around the room, I could tell his motor was still running at high speed, even though he made a valiant attempt to rein it in. We chatted for a while, and the sparks began flying as we discussed a local political issue. I could still sense the fire burning just below the surface, even though he had been retired for several years. I wondered at the time if part of the retirement adjustment problem could be caused by personality type.

After my retirement, I got involved in every aspect of running the house, which had previously been my wife's domain. You can imagine how well that went over. Then I invested a great deal of time outdoors working around the property, painting and fixing things. I discovered that I dislike repairing things and don't look forward to doing yard work. I receive no pleasure from either. On top of that, I irritated an old back injury and ended up at a surgical clinic in Tampa, Florida. Fortunately, I found alternative treatment, but one could literally say that retirement was becoming a pain in my backside. Of course, during this time I read every book I'd had on my "must read" list for the past five years. I love to read—it's a passion of mine—but enough was enough. When winter came,

I started climbing the walls. I wondered what people do when they retire and cannot go outside. My answer was, and still is, they implode. I booked a trip to Florida in order to break the monotony of the dreary winter months. In the spring, I decided I needed a challenge, something to look forward to. So I bought a Fuji Monterey trail bike and started training for a long bike trip that would take me from Cumberland, Maryland, to Pittsburgh, Pennsylvania, along the Great Allegheny Passage. The incredibly beautiful bike trail I traveled on runs alongside the Chesapeake and Ohio Canal. This three-day bike trip is referred to in the family as "Robert's Great Adventure." I departed the first week of October along with two family members, who, I suspect, accompanied me in case I had a coronary and needed emergency assistance. The first day we rode forty-two miles uphill at a slight incline the entire way. The second day we covered fifty-two miles, which was my absolute physical limit. On the third day, after riding only a few miles, the trail stopped in McKeesport, Pennsylvania, because it had not been completed all the way into Pittsburgh. Exhausted, we turned around, but during the ride home I realized how much satisfaction I felt achieving goals and expending great effort. However, I also understood that it was not feasible to take a one-hundred-mile bike trip every time I needed a challenge or something to do.

After some serious soul searching, motivated by my continuing discomfort, I decided to confront the issue and look more deeply into myself. I wanted to understand why this transition to retirement was so difficult. What was preventing my adjustment to a new "downsized" life? Then I remembered the Enneagram—which is a powerful tool for identifying distinctive personality characteristics—and wondered if it might provide a key to the puzzle.

Chapter 2

Identifying Your Enneagram Type

According to a recent article in the *Journal of Employee Assistance*, becoming a retiree usually affects four areas of a person's life: the financial, social, family, and psychological.[1] Each of these areas can act as a potential land mine and create major problems for the retiree. Retirement means saying goodbye to a work life and all of its complexities and challenges. It also requires the loosening of social ties that may have provided a sense of identity and separation from coworkers who may have provided great enjoyment. It may also entail adapting to a smaller budget with fewer trips and entertainment options. Add in the fact that a growing percentage of all retirements are involuntary, meaning the individual was not given the opportunity to choose the date and time of his or her retirement. Organizations find it more acceptable to

---

1. Andrea Lardani and Raul Correa, "A Preventive Approach to Retirement," *Journal of Employee Assistance*, March 2005, http://findarticles.com/p/articles/mi_m0PLP/is_1_35/ai_n17208168/.

11

offer "early outs" for their older employees. In effect, the message is: "take this exit package or risk eventual termination with fewer benefits." For these individuals, no time or planning is available to prepare for this major life transition.

Navigating these changes requires psychological flexibility that may not exist within the retiree and the retiree's family members. For most people, managing change when you are in your sixties can be more difficult than at age thirty. For those with an achievement addiction, change can be catastrophic due to the immense psychological stress created by these uncontrollable life-changing events. Few are as fortunate as Valentino, the famous fashion designer, who commented upon his retirement, "I was proud to stop at the right moment while the room was full."

Other research has shown that retirement distress may occur at different intervals. For example, many retirees report great happiness and satisfaction during the first six to twelve months of retirement—referred to as "the honeymoon period"—only to feel distress at a later time.[2] These individuals learn that it only takes a short time to do all the things they dreamed about once they have freedom from their working life. They wonder, "What's next? Is that all there is?"

In my own case, that is exactly what happened; the first several months of my retirement were a novel experience for me. It was the first time in thirty-seven

---

2. Michael D. Davies, "The Psychological Adjustment to Relocation Following Retirement" (dissertation, Griffith University, 2003), 4.

years I did not have time restraints or a structured routine. I didn't have to be anywhere or do anything I did not want to do. This eventually led me into a phase I refer to as "the dead zone." I entered a long period where nothing was particularly pleasurable for me. It wasn't a terribly painful time, but it was uncomfortable enough for me to know that something was wrong. I simply concluded that I was not happy with my new life—there wasn't enough going on that interested me.

After undergoing that soul-searching process, reviewing research on retirement satisfaction, and listening to many retirees discuss their own adjustment challenges, I now believe that a person's unique personality type, powered by an achievement addiction, is the biggest cause of problems adjusting to retirement.

I have come to learn that different people process life-changing events in various ways, depending upon their personality type. You slam a hard-charging personality type with an achievement addiction into an unplanned, downsized retirement life and you won't see stress like this unless you invested your retirement money with Bernie Madoff. Understanding your personality type, whether or not you have an achievement addiction, provides the necessary tools for you to gain deeper insight into the unique personality attributes that could cause you conflict and unhappiness. This increased knowledge will enable you to chart a course in retirement that fits your specific personality profile, hopefully resulting in increased joy and satisfaction.

I first discovered the Enneagram in the late 1980s when I read the book *The Enneagram: Understanding Yourself and the Others in Your Life* by Helen Palmer. I recall being very impressed by the depth of knowledge provided by this system for describing personality types. During my graduate studies in psychology, I was exposed to every type of analysis one can imagine. There were times when I felt like a lab rat because I completed so many psychological questionnaires that described my personality. As a result of those experiences, I thought I knew myself rather well—until I started studying the Enneagram. I discovered that it brought my self-knowledge to a higher and more comprehensive level.

I know the Enneagram Types (E-Types) of all of my family members and have used them throughout my business career. They have always provided valuable information and increased my self-understanding as well as that of my close associates. It came as a recent revelation to me that I could also use them to achieve a more successful and fulfilling retirement.

As a first step, let's identify your E-Type. Please be aware that there is much more to the Enneagram methodology than you will learn in this book. We are going to be very pragmatic and use it for our retirement planning purposes only. I have listed references in the Recommended Reading section at the end of the book if you care to learn more about the Enneagram.

The Enneagram has a rather mysterious history. There are some who believe it was created by the Sufis as part of their esoteric oral tradition and revealed to the world by the Armenian mystic George Gurdjieff. Others believe Oscar Ichazo, a Bolivian psychotherapist who founded the Arica School in Chile, conceived it. Ichazo most likely integrated the Sufi wisdom he garnered during his travels throughout Asia into a more formal model for understanding personality. Enneagram methodology is characterized by a circular diagram on which personality types are symbolically represented at nine points around the circumference. Arrows reveal the personality types, their adjoining influences, and interconnections with other types.

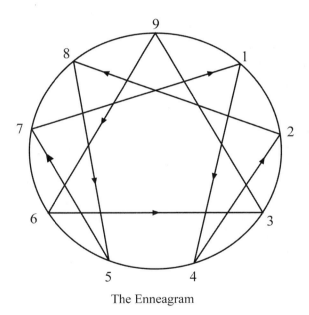

The Enneagram

Each E-Type is represented as functioning along a continuum somewhere between health (integration) and neurosis (disintegration). Although we possess some of the characteristics of all nine types within us, through our genetics and early environment we have chosen to adopt one of the types for our primary pattern of behavior. Your E-Type reveals the underlying propensities that guide and influence your behavior. In the majority of instances I have witnessed, these behavioral descriptions come as somewhat of a surprise to those first learning their E-Type. In summary, the Enneagram enables you to gain knowledge of your true self, exposing the hidden motivations for actions and illusions that you employ in your daily life.

The Formation of Type

You entered this world and were introduced to a large number of influences and circumstances that fluctuated and varied. Life was already well underway with the routine of your mother and other caregivers. You were integrated into this moving and shifting environment and had to adapt to the reality you encountered. All you knew at the time was that you had primal needs such as touch, food, interaction, and love that had to be met. You were helpless to satisfy your own needs and were completely dependent upon those around you for your care. When you felt this loving care it brought you immense joy and satisfaction, but most importantly you felt secure. As time went on and your needs continued to be satisfied, you gained confidence in the world around you believing it was trustworthy and benevolent. In addition, you gained confidence that you could control your little world because when you cried someone came to feed, change, or hold you. You were never abandoned or neglected in any way and so you grew into a resilient, strong, and healthy adult. If this describes your early childhood, consider yourself blessed, because these consistently positive conditions are extremely rare.

How do people raised in a highly responsive and supportive setting see the world? What do they need? Abraham Maslow, the famed psychologist, performed the definitive study on this type of person. Dr. George Boeree, Professor of Psychology at Shippensburg University, lists the following needs as stated by these self-actualized individuals:

Truth, rather than dishonesty

Goodness, rather than evil

Beauty, not ugliness or vulgarity

Unity, wholeness, and transcendence of opposites, not arbitrariness or forced choices

Aliveness, not deadness or the mechanization of life

Uniqueness, not bland uniformity

Perfection and necessity, not sloppiness, inconsistency, or accident

Completion, rather than incompleteness

Justice and order, not injustice and lawlessness

Simplicity, not unnecessary complexity

Richness, not environmental impoverishment

Effortlessness, not strain

Playfulness, not grim, humorless, drudgery

17

Self-sufficiency, not dependency

Meaningfulness, rather than senselessness

These needs may seem perfectly normal to a self-actualized individual, but they aren't standard for everyone. The primary reason for this is that a person needs to trust the workings of the universe or divine flow of life to be sensitive to and attracted to these needs. If you went into the ghettos of major cities and asked those you encountered what they needed for happiness, I doubt many of these items would be mentioned. If people are struggling for survival or down on their luck, other needs take precedence.

Another key attribute of these self-actualized individuals is their calm acceptance of life. They do not fight with the world around them but tend to go along with life's momentum and flow with the current of unfolding events. I point this out because these individuals seldom become achievement addicts for the simple reason they move with the flow of divine energy and have no deeply embedded needs driving them to conquer and achieve. If anything, they may appear passive and ascetic simply because they are happy people and do not make great demands on their immediate environment. Why work until midnight on a deal when you can listen to music or walk in the woods and be filled with ecstasy?

Truthfully, these are not the nation builders and top executives of the world. They already have what everyone else is striving for—inner peace supported by a strong spiritual connection to the divine.

Now that we know what perfection looks like—
what does it mean for us, the sorry souls with an
achievement addiction blindly milling around in
the dark? As we learned, we constructed our world-
view during the first four to five years of our lives.
What happens if our early environment was not perfect, if it had some kinks in it? Our parents had
their own stresses and conflicts to manage when we
entered their lives as infants. Our own mothers, who
most likely have an imprint on their psyches from
being raised by imperfect parents, may very well
have handed down this legacy to us for better or for
worse. As a result, as a small child you may have
been subjected to inconsistent nurturing. If you
were fortunate, your needs were mostly satisfied,
but with wide variability; if you were less fortunate,
you were raised in a state of constant deprivation.
Based on the unique pattern of your early environment, you made a critical decision—you could not
completely trust the world around you to fulfill your
needs. You were forced to react to this early environment in order to secure your own welfare and
protection. To quote A. H. Almaas in his book *Facets of Unity: The Enneagram of Holy Ideas*: "Without
basic trust, we don't have trust in our nature, our
inner resources, and in the universe that gave birth
to us and is constantly supporting us, constantly
providing for us, and will continue providing for us
whatever we really need."[3]

---

3. Almaas, *Facets of Unity*, 30.

Without basic trust, you could not count on things working out, and were left feeling at a loss and insufficient. You had to make some personal adjustments because you lost confidence in the reliability of your caregivers. You could not always take your vital safety and security for granted—things were not automatically provided for you without effort on your part. When you looked out over your immediate circumstances you made the determination that you did not always get the love and attention you needed when you needed it. Rather than trusting in the divine flow (God, Tao, Buddha mind, universal consciousness, spiritual energy field), you had to make changes to make things right. At this point you lost your innocence. Without basic trust you became more reluctant to take risks; feelings of hopelessness arose, and you lost your ability to relax. Possibly you decided you had to withdraw or make it on your own. Life became work. You projected your understanding of life as you experienced it in childhood onto your adult world. This became your own unique code of conduct. Most importantly, you seriously weakened or severed your connection with the divine energy field, which is the primary source of true happiness.

This loss is not unique to you but is the general human condition. Unless you are one of Maslow's self-actualized people, you experienced need deprivation to some degree. The only variation is the extent of your deprivation in childhood and your specific decision of how best to cope with it. You had several behavioral alternatives available to you: (1) try to be perfect; (2)

become more loving and attentive so that you receive more love and attention in return; (3) draw attention to yourself through your accomplishments; (4) become angry and complain; (5) withdraw emotionally and disconnect from the pain; (6) become cautious, fearful, and suspicious, and hunker down; (7) act out and attract attention; (8) become angry and demanding; or (9) fade into transparency and make no waves. The behavior you chose at that early age represents your E-Type.

Your particular type describes how you have chosen to be in the world. You formed your personality, possibly through trial and error, at a premature age in order to cope with the contingencies encountered in the early childhood environment. What was the best course of action for you to take? Your needs were simple and basic. You could either make every effort to get them met or withdraw and form a protective shield to minimize the hurt caused by deprivation. Your decision structured the general personality framework and architecture you now use to travel through life.

It is now time to identify your E-Type. What follows is a brief description of each of the nine personality types. Please read each one carefully and try to identify the E-Type that best describes you. Don't be concerned if you identify with more than one type. If you are uncertain after reading these descriptions do not despair, a questionnaire is provided in Appendix A to help you confirm your choice.

E-Type 1: The Master

You are a perfectionist at heart. You have great interest in detail and like to solve problems and fix things. Your cars are always spotless and polished, your shoes are shined, and your clothes are usually clean and pressed. You care about your appearance and like to be well-groomed. You receive pleasure from improving things around you and take great pride in your mastery over those areas in your life that are important. You tend to be tense and have difficulty relaxing before you accomplish everything on your to-do list. You are always tinkering with things and have a deep understanding and appreciation of how things work. You are attracted to professions, such as engineering, where you can design and build things. You are extremely meticulous and like to do everything yourself because no one can meet your high standards of perfection. You are not a good delegator. You are very dependable, hard working, and efficient, and view the world through rules and regulations. You are highly respectful of the authority figures in your life. You tend to be controlling and slightly rigid in your thinking. You are highly analytical and secretly feel superior because of your high standards. You can be excessively critical of yourself and others, domineering, extremely demanding, and angry, but you try hard to suppress it. You can rub people the wrong way. You resent others who get ahead without sacrifice and commitment. You seldom meet people who you believe are as capable as you. You have the capacity to experience great pleasure and satisfaction, particularly if you believe it is well earned. You have a tendency to overwork and devote too much time to your career. Unhappiness stems from your perspective that most things in your life require a great deal of effort and attention to be acceptable, including yourself.

E-Type 2: The Enchanter

To you, relationships are the most important thing in your life. You have the unique ability to get other people to like you, by basically changing yourself and becoming whatever is most acceptable to them. You intuitively know what to do and what to say to lure an unsuspecting person into a relationship. You are often the "power behind the throne" of authority figures. You are a warm, tender, and supportive person capable of great caring and empathy. You make a wonderful and attentive spouse and friend. You are focused on feeling and you have a very romantic view of life. You may read romance novels to satisfy a vicarious need for more love and passion in your life. Others may see you as living in la-la land, not interested or knowledgeable of current events, but you know every anniversary and birthday in your family by heart. You actively keep in touch with friends and family via e-mail, cards on special occasions, and phone conversations. You usually know everything that is going on, in detail, within your network of relationships. You like children and enjoy caring for and interacting with them. You have a tendency to get your own way through manipulation and seduction. You often give to others with the hidden intent of getting something in return. This is usually an unconscious motive that surfaces when you feel that you give more than you receive. On these occasions you complain, become frustrated, and feel a sense of betrayal and resentfulness. Feelings of ungratefulness can be a common emotion. You have a stubborn streak that is unshakable and you do not like to deviate from routine. Control over others is achieved through your helpfulness. You can make yourself indispensable to those around you, which is a form of security, control, and power. One of your most important goals is to be needed by others. It is easy for you to be aware and sensitive to the needs of others, but you often struggle when trying to establish a clear understanding of your own needs. More than anything you value feelings of love, security, and romance.

E-Type 3: The Star

You are an individual with strong achievement motivation who gravitates toward leadership. You are charming, cheerful, optimistic, and action oriented. You work hard and assume leadership roles in order to win in a competitive world. Your primary motivation is to avoid failure and be a success. You exude feelings of confidence and well-being, which attracts others to you. You look and act like a winner. If you are a housewife, you are the president of the garden club; if you are a businessperson, you are the CEO, senior executive, or general partner of a firm. You usually earn a good living. You are image conscious and marketing oriented. You have the ability to influence others and have good intuition regarding how to succeed. You are easily identifiable because you are always striving and busy. Your calendar is full of meetings and commitments. You are always on the go and focused on the outside world. You are challenged by meeting all of your commitments. You seldom take the time to reflect, and when you do, it makes you uncomfortable. You are socially skilled, attract attention, and can become a performer when the occasion calls for it. You take your computer and cell phone with you on vacation and secretly find doing a deal or taking calls from the office more pleasurable than actually spending time with your family. You portray an idealized image to others by living in the right neighborhood, with good-looking, high-achieving children, and an attractive spouse. You are drawn to and value success above everything else and surround yourself with friends and associates who share similar views. Your self-worth depends more upon what you do rather than who you are, and you tend to be disconnected from your inner self. You can change into whatever you need to be in order to win. This chameleon-like quality can trouble you, and you may wonder if you are betraying yourself on some occasions. You can take an idea and move quickly and directly into action. You are willing to take on authority figures if required to make progress. You are efficient, precise in your actions, and totally committed to success; however, deep inside you are more dedicated to the process than the outcome. You enjoy the recognition associated with accomplishment, but more than anything, you want to be a winner.

E-Type 4: The Drama Queen

You live your life swinging between exhilaration and depression. You are elegant, stylish, and sensitive with a flair for the dramatic. You are passionate, impulsive, and subject to severe mood swings. You can be a sensual lover one minute and a disapproving critic the next. You have a profound artistic nature and often can be seen as a "tortured soul." Your feelings are highly sensitive and you can be hurt simply by a small glance or gesture. You feel rejection deeply. You are devilish by nature and do not conform to authority unless it is of the highest order. You can be extremely interesting while at the same time maddening. You often feel like a victim of life and become morose and self-destructive. You are cynical by nature and have little faith in the goodness of others. You take on a "poor me" attitude and have a habit of rejecting whatever is easy to obtain. Deep intimacy is threatening to you because it makes you feel inadequate, as though something inside of you is missing. You prefer to keep relationships at arm's length. You romanticize those you want to attract, and then reject them once their flaws become evident. Your customary mood is one of melancholy. You actually enjoy music, movies, books, and plays that offer a degree of wistful sadness. You have a heightened sensitivity to other people's emotions and pain and can be highly supportive of them in crisis. You have a temperamental connection to intense emotion. You may have a deep commitment to religion, spirituality, and metaphysics. You occasionally overwhelm others with your strong passions and emotional outbursts. You cannot seem to relinquish the depth of suffering. In this state you can be pessimistic, skeptical, somber, irritable, complaining, despondent, critical, bitter, self-defeating, and vain—and that's just for starters. You can also be extremely interesting, fun, passionate, unique, clever, sensual, erotic, and noble. Your inner life can be characterized as searching for something that is missing—a feeling of being disconnected or unable to grasp something that you desperately need—which manifests as emotional conflicts and vivid drama.

E-Type 5: The Solitary Mystic

Above all else you seek solitude. You live a life of independence and choose sovereignty over attachment. You may live in a remote area. You reject dependency on anyone or anything and will not work in an environment that is hostile, closely controlled, or artificial. You may be self-employed. If required, you can shrink your personal needs down to a minimalist lifestyle without viewing it as a significant sacrifice. You do not like having your time confiscated by obligations or other people's schedules. You love to read, ponder abstract concepts, and think deeply about nature. You can investigate arcane topics and become an expert in those areas of interest with little or no contact with the outside world. You will often surprise people with the depth and breadth of your knowledge on particular subjects. You live mainly in your head and attempt to limit emotional involvement as much as possible. You seldom reveal personal information to strangers. You have a few select friends that you value highly, provided they grant you the freedom to come and go. You usually share a special bond with these select individuals because you have special interests in common. You are exceptionally loyal to the few friends that you treasure. You seldom require the spotlight and prefer to be the power behind the scenes. You can be invaluable to authority figures because of your ability to detach and look at things in depth with objectivity. You are a great scholar, teacher, writer, or inventor, and tend to be attracted to subjects considered New Age, such as metaphysics. What others consider far out, you consider mainstream and common sense. At both family and social gatherings, you tend to be uncomfortable and can't wait to depart. You seldom work the room but instead seek out an interesting person or make yourself cleverly invisible. You process your emotions in private and can enjoy reviewing social interactions after they have occurred in the privacy of your thoughts. You are not extemporaneous and prefer speaking on a topic once you have given it a great deal of thought. You may love pets because you receive affection without onerous expectations and emotional entanglements. You are indifferent to praise and recognition from others and maintain a detached perspective regarding most things in your life. When you become angry, you are seldom confrontational; rather, you withdraw into a cold silence and sulk. You can maintain this icy silence longer than expected. Rather than resolve a conflict through dialogue and emotional expression, you think your way through it by analyzing and compartmentalizing the issue until it is completely understood and resolved in your mind. Only then are you capable of moving toward reconciliation. In matters of money, you are apt to be very conservative and instinctively hoard your resources, so that your independence cannot be threatened. When you are engaged in work or social activities for an extended period of time, you require private time alone to recharge your batteries. You are rarely bored because you have nothing to do. There is so much to explore and learn. In a moment of honesty, you may admit feeling a sense of superiority over others because of the extent of your knowledge or because you need less than they do to be happy.

E-Type 6: The Closet Rebel

You are suspicious by nature and attracted to underdog causes. You work best in environments that are orderly, predictable, structured, and routine. You are cautious and socially inhibited but can exert tremendous energy to any project that you believe in. You follow strong, compassionate leaders and can be extremely loyal to your employer, provided that fairness and honesty are practiced at all times. You are well known for having a good "BS detector," and you become very suspicious of those you believe are dishonest or hustlers. You tend toward procrastination, particularly at the end of projects. When evaluating issues, you will identify everything that could go wrong without expressing confidence in the outcome. You are cynical by nature and can be characterized by H. L. Mencken's definition of a cynic, "A cynic is a man who, when he smells flowers, looks around for the coffin." You have a rebellious streak that often goes unnoticed by your friends and coworkers because you keep it well hidden from view. You can be attracted to gurus, anti-establishment provocateurs, and those who resist conventional wisdom. Above all you want to feel safe and secure. You constantly monitor your immediate environment for anything that could be harmful. You are loyal, analytical, dutiful, precise, hardworking, punctual, and a good critical thinker and problem solver. You are particularly adept at identifying problems that could go wrong at the beginning of any venture. You have problems submitting to authority and can become passive-aggressive when being challenged. You can only work for someone you trust. You may be attracted to self-employment, so that you can exert more control over authority relationships. You can frustrate loved ones with your skepticism and doubt regarding change and new initiatives. You are usually well informed on subjects that matter, and those close to you respect your opinion. What you need most is to align with a cause or organizational leader that is just and honorable.

E-Type 7: The Cruise Director

You are optimistic by nature and have an upbeat personality. You are charming and a terrific networker. People gravitate to you because of your charisma, bright outlook, and adventuresome demeanor. You like to go places and do things—the more the better. You look forward to fun-filled outings with much anticipation. You seldom feel the emotion of fear. Life is full of interesting possibilities and you want to partake in each and every one of them. You keep multiple options open and are highly flexible in your approach to life. If something does not work out, you do not get depressed but simply shift over to another track of entertaining experience. You love Disney World. You have an active imagination and vivid fantasy life. You would make a terrific children's author, fiction novelist, salesperson, or real estate agent. You enjoy planning and hosting social events, such as birthdays and anniversaries. You have good taste and enjoy sampling the best the world has to offer. You are a passionate traveler and have interesting memories and artifacts collected from romantic locales. You have visionary plans for the future that are extremely exciting. You need to maintain high levels of stimulation because you can quickly lose interest if things are not fun and interesting. You are much better at visualizing, planning, and organizing a project than you are doing the day-to-day detailed work required for successful completion. You do not like to get bogged down in details and drudgery. You like to fly above the clouds and zoom in whenever the mood needs to be elevated. You lift the spirits of those around you and help others see the possibilities in any situation. You believe that you can talk your way out of most difficult situations because you are charming and quick-witted. You do not like authority that is unreasonable and will quickly exit any environment that is too controlling, heavy-handed, or rule governed. You have a weakness for overindulgence, and occasionally take on too much activity without anticipating the consequences. Under stress you become irritable, restless, and overconfident. At your worst you are self-indulgent. However, your moodiness does not last long because it is very easy for you to find new challenges and adventures. You do not do well with boring routine and excel in activities where there is freedom of movement, either physically or intellectually. Above all you need play.

E-Type 8: The Conquistador

You gravitate toward power and control. You have a need to take charge and be a leader. You are a natural at confronting obstacles and taking action. You can move mountains once you are committed to a goal. You are not particularly introspective, and few people really know your inner self. You see yourself as a protector of those less powerful or fortunate. You do not trust anyone who will not fight for his or her strongly held beliefs. You are extremely comfortable with confrontation and believe that it is the most effective way to get at the truth. You are often not aware that others are intimidated by your behavior and dislike your direct approach. You do not respect weakness. You have an expanded sense of self and believe you are physically powerful. You believe that only the strong survive. When you become angry you feel as though your body grows larger and more powerful. You will fight to the death in an argument and often weaken your opponents through sheer willpower. You seldom back down. You get into trouble when you become bored. You will pick a fight to make things interesting, or you will go to the extreme through excessive spending, overeating, binge drinking, or lustfulness. You are predatory by nature and want to gain complete control over your environment. You like to break the rules to see what happens. You often function as if rules were made for other people. You flourish in the atmosphere of open competition. Seldom are others willing to sacrifice as much as you to win. You overcome barriers through sheer force of will. You feel secure only when you are calling the shots and in control. You dislike injustice and will come to the aggressive defense of those being persecuted. You are softhearted toward friends and those in your sphere of influence. You tend to see things in terms of black and white. You seldom feel fear and become anxious only when you have not identified the weaknesses of your opponents. You can become ruthless when you feel vulnerable. While you are functioning in your comfort zone most others around you can feel deeply threatened and stressed. If you were a toy you would be an action hero. If you were a TV personality you would be Bill O'Reilly. Your greatest weaknesses are insensitivity, impatience, self-centeredness, and hyperactivity. Most of all, you need a castle.

E-Type 9: The Harmonizer

You can clearly see both sides of any issue. You are a great friend and can listen and be very helpful in times of need. You have good insight into the inner world of those close to you and are sought out for advice and counsel. You are inherently a good person, generous, kind, modest, contented, peaceful, humorous, and softhearted. You are dependable, stable, reliable, unpretentious, and nurturing. Most of all you are well-balanced. You love animals and nature. You are attracted to jobs that require attention to detail and structured routine. You excel in any position that requires you to put things into order, such as accounting and office administration. You thrive in a bureaucracy. You are a supportive and loving spouse. You are a well-known procrastinator and easily become diverted by trivial things and lose sight of important tasks. You often put off a critical task to the end of the day and then forget about it. You have difficulty saying no and struggle with decision-making. It is easier for you to help a friend make a decision than it is for you to know the best course of action for yourself. You can stay in a suspended state of uncertainty for a long time without making an important decision and taking appropriate action. You can become very stubborn when others try to help you with a decision. You have a long list of rituals that function much like a narcotic, such as cleaning closets, endless hours of watching TV, and other acts of diversion. These obsessive activities are used to prevent you from addressing important life issues. An independent observer would say that you spend all day on unimportant things and little or no time on matters that improve your life. You have an overreliance on other people and leach their energy and ambition. You need friends and loved ones to initiate social activities so that you can go along. You assimilate their interests and priorities into your life without considering your own needs and opinions. You are more of a follower than a leader. When you become angry you are passive-aggressive. You can hold grievances inside for a long period and then explode. On these rare occasions it feels good to finally make a strong statement on your own behalf. You are weak-willed and often give up on resolving frustrations and conflicts until everything breaks down. This can lead to depression. You are overly sensitive to criticism and are lacking in self-confidence. You could be extremely handsome or beautiful and still feel insecure regarding your appearance. You are physically active but complacent by nature and lack focused energy. More than anything you need love and greater self-awareness.

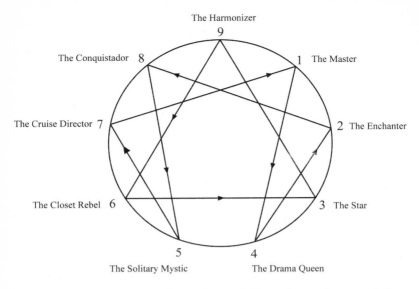

At this point you have hopefully selected one of the E-Types and feel confident that it accurately describes your personality. You may not share all of the qualities described for your type due to the fact that very healthy individuals often have less of the negative and more of the positive qualities, while less healthy individuals frequently have more of the negative and possibly less of the positive qualities. The type you have selected should describe you in general. Possibly you are unsure which type best describes you. If so, please go to Appendix A and fill out the E-Type Questionnaire. It will help you make your choice. Your true type should be included in your highest two or three scores. I also recommend talking with loved ones and close friends and asking them for their opinion. You may be surprised at how well they know the real you. Do not continue on to chapter 3 until you have made a final decision.

Chapter 3

Charting Your Course in Retirement

What makes retirement adjustment difficult for some people is the fact that every human being is unique. I have learned from my own experience that one size does not fit all when it comes to charting a successful retirement strategy. In fact, many people hate the term "retirement" because they find that it has the connotation of being over the hill, when they are in fact eagerly looking forward to many active and challenging years. The basic premise of this book is that there are different natural talents and abilities for different types of people; they have varied interests and proclivities based upon their personality type. Without this fundamental understanding, you can wander aimlessly through your retirement years in a frustrating attempt to find your path to happiness. Eventually, through painful trial and error, you will either find your way to contentment or become resigned to a life lacking zest and joie de vivre. It may take years of trying various activities before stumbling upon the right course of action. This can be a long and painful period of adjustment because it feels as though you are navigating uncharted waters.

When I was in the midst of my own somewhat painful retirement transition, I spoke with a good friend who is a clinical psychologist living in Atlanta, Georgia. He had recently lost his wife to cancer and we had spoken a few times in the previous months about our life-changing events. During one of our phone conversations he asked me how I was doing in retirement. Normally, when asked this question, I offer the white lie that I was fine and enjoying life. However, I have always been open and truthful with him, so I said that I felt lost and lacked direction. I think this was one of the few times I was totally honest with anyone other than my wife and another very close friend about my situation.

It is not easy for me to admit problems or weaknesses to others, no matter how close a friend. But it had been well over a year since I had retired and my discomfort level did not seem to be improving. He said, "Why don't you think about those things that you have done in the past that were successful and that gave you pleasure? This should give you some direction as to what you should be doing in retirement." I hung up the phone and started to think about what those words really meant.

The more I thought about it, the more this suggestion made sense. I considered many alternatives and arrived at one set of four interconnected activities that met the criteria of things I have done successfully in the past. They were as follows:

- Conceiving new ideas that were interesting to me and beneficial to others.

- Building out the ideas into prototypes or models.

- Presenting the prototypes or models to others and discussing their value.

- Earning monetary rewards based on the value and contribution of the ideas.

I had the sense that these activities were perfectly compatible with my E-Type personality, which is E-Type 5: The Solitary Mystic. If you will recall, this type can be characterized by loving to dream up new ideas, research, and think deeply about topics of interest, some of which could be considered unconventional. This type has extremely good intuition and can discover trends before they become mainstream. Working alone for long periods of time in deep contemplation poses no problem, nor does speaking to others in a persuasive fashion on topics that have been thoroughly researched. Money is attractive to The Solitary Mystic because it represents freedom from dependency and outside interference. It occurred to me that these activities may not be appropriate for another E-Type, but they were perfect for me.

My conversation also triggered the idea that the concept of miniaturization could potentially be extremely beneficial when planning retirement. Could I take the things I had been good at, which were compatible with my E-Type, and miniaturize them in retirement? In other words, could the processes and activities of my working life be employed in my retirement life, only on a smaller scale? I believe that personal fulfillment depends more upon the context of our life rather than its content. For example, if you were an excellent administrative manager for a Fortune 500 company, you may receive satisfaction from employing some of those same management skills for a much smaller enterprise, such as a church, school, political group, or start-up business.

Malcolm Gladwell's book *Outliers: The Story of Success* introduces the notion of time of practice, or how long it takes to really get good at something. Consider those tasks on which you spent the majority of your time prior to your retirement. The research indicates that it takes more than ten thousand hours of practice to become highly skilled at a task. This equates to three hours of practice every day over a period of ten years.

Gladwell quotes neurologist Daniel Levitin as follows:

In study after study, of composers, basketball players, fiction writers, ice-skaters, concert pianists, chess players, master criminals, this number comes up again and again. Ten thousand hours is equivalent to roughly three hours a day, or 20 hours a week, of practice over 10 years...It seems that it takes the brain this long to assimilate all that it needs to know to achieve true mastery.[1]

The tasks where you have spent the greatest amount of your time are where you will find your greatest skill. This is not to suggest that you should not explore new areas of interest in retirement, only that you may have honed a set of skills through thousands of hours of practice during your working career that could be employed during your retirement, primarily because of your proficiency level and the satisfaction you receive from performing the tasks. Of course, you may have spent years developing a high level of expertise in work that did not give you pleasure. If this is the case, you should explore other areas of interest.

It is evident that high-risk retirees who transition into retirement with increased self-awareness through knowledge of their E-Types have a better chance of successfully managing their life choices after retirement than those who do not. Therefore, the following sections recommend post-retirement activities based on the distinctive nature and unique attributes of each E-Type. Please keep in mind these are only general recommendations for you to consider. Now turn to the section that follows and review the Activity Map for your particular E-Type. Your map provides a listing of potential retirement activities that match your specific E-Type. You will notice that several maps have retirement stories of individuals that share your particular type.

---

1. Gladwell, *Outliers*, 40.

ACTIVITY MAP

E-Type 1: The Master

The essence of The Master is the desire for precision and perfection. This individual likes to fix, analyze, design, and build things.

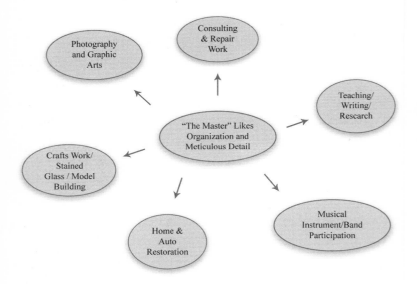

All of the Enneagram types can experience adjustment problems in retirement primarily due to their level of performance addiction; however, some of the types, just by their intrinsic nature, are at higher risk for more severe psychological disruption. As an E-Type 1: The Master, you have a very high risk of depression and maladjustment during the early and middle stages of retirement because of your driven personality, controlling nature, and desire for perfection. If possible it would be beneficial for you to ease into retirement by working part-time, or have projects planned where there is a passion for the work. Pursuing hobbies that have been long delayed due to work commitments, as well as consulting, part-time teaching, research, and writing, are activities well suited to this E-Type. More than anything, you need beauty.

The Story of B

I first met B when my firm was bidding on a government contract to build an online communications system that distributed the U.S. Department of Transportation's drug regulations throughout the country. This was a large-system application where transportation workers could contact the system and request regulatory information either by phone, fax, or modem.

B was a stout woman with a twinkle in her eye, who was born in Montana where she was taught to shoot a rifle before her eleventh birthday. She had a plainswoman persona and exuded honesty, strength, and commitment. She had entered civil service as a clerk typist and worked her way up to a GS 15 level position. As a senior manager she took personal responsibility for the success of our project in every way possible. That's when I learned she was an E-Type 1: The Master. We had well over five thousand pages of documents in our computer system and she personally read and edited each one. She would troubleshoot the system long into the night and call me early in the morning with her report. She called our office every day to discuss the system operation and became a driving force in our pursuit of excellence. On Monday mornings she would call in to discuss her weekend review; often she wanted to speak directly to the programmers working on the system. Her attention to detail was amazing to everyone on our team and occasionally embarrassing because she would find deeply embedded programming bugs that our own staff had overlooked. We were not sure we would ever receive her final approval. We came to the realization that it would not happen until she felt the system was perfect in every way. She invested so much time and energy into the development of the system that she won the respect and admiration of every member of our design team.

After the system had been operational for several months, a change in administrations occurred in Washington and a political decision was made to shut the system down. B could not understand how this decision could be made, particularly given the system's high utilization rate. It made her furious. Nevertheless, a few weeks after the plug was pulled B announced her retirement—she was through with government service. Rather than remain in Washington D.C., she decided to sell her condominium and move back to Montana. Her son, who was a builder, constructed a log home for her on a mountain adjacent to the Continental Divide. It seemed like a perfect way to retire.

For the first year she seemed to be happy living so close to nature. She cared for her brother who was stricken with cancer and provided him with financial assistance. She continued to pursue her interest in computers and was an avid Internet user. Suddenly, during one of our phone conversations she said, "Bob, if you dare tell anyone this I will kill you, but I made a big mistake coming out here. I should have stayed in Washington D.C." It was unlike B to ever show weakness of any kind or admit a mistake. For her to make this statement to me meant that she had felt terribly unhappy, distressed, isolated, and alienated living so far away from her old life. A few months later I learned from her that she had undergone major surgery for cancer. And a few months after that, I received an e-mail from her son stating that she had passed away. I realized that the only thing that B did not do expertly was make good decisions about her retirement based on sound knowledge of her unique and rather glorious personality.

Now go to chapter 4.

ACTIVITY MAP

E-Type 2: The Enchanter

The Enchanter wants to feel needed and forms a close emotional attachment to others.

All of the Enneagram types can experience adjustment problems in retirement primarily due to their level of performance addiction; however, some of the types, just by their intrinsic nature, may be at higher risk for psychological disruption. As an E-Type 2: The

Enchanter, you are only moderately susceptible to depression and emotional stress during the early and middle stages of retirement because of your large network of friends and family and your unique ability to maintain long-standing relationships. No other E-Type places as much emphasis on personal relationships as The Enchanter. If, however, close personal friendships are lost due to retirement separation, emotional stress could be experienced. It would be beneficial for you to make a special effort to stay in close contact with your work associates after retirement. More than anything you need love.

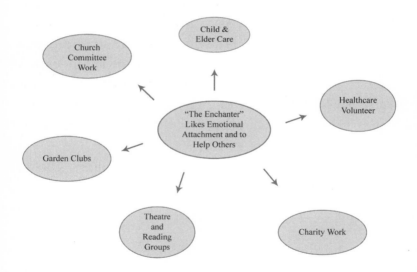

The Story of L

L retired after a successful career as a speech pathologist, special education teacher, and school administrator. As an administrator in a special education center, she was responsible for overseeing many of the programs implemented by one-hundred-and-thirty staff members for six-hundred students. She possesses a BS in speech pathology and a master's in special education. She won a coveted "Teacher of the Year" award for the entire county school system while teaching in the classroom. She describes herself as somewhat of a perfectionist who devoted much of her time and attention as an administrator and teacher to ensuring that she performed in a highly effective fashion. She observes, "Sometimes I was too dedicated and committed to my job and missed out on some enjoyable activities with family and friends. My husband helped me to see the value of living a more balanced life, particularly toward the end of my career." The fact that she was considered a distinguished member of the educational leadership team and was highly successful in attaining her career goals, has given her a sense of ongoing satisfaction during her retirement years.

When she retired, she and her husband, who is also a retired educator, decided to move to a resort community within close driving distance to the beach. Purchasing a new home gave her a sense of purpose and joy during the early months of her retirement. She said, "Moving was a good decision for us. We had made the decision prior to my retirement and it was not done on the spur of the moment. I wanted to make a fresh start in a new community away from my old life. I think we just wanted to try something new and different."

When you speak with L, you come away with the feeling that she is a good planner—that she thinks things through before acting and likes to get things done. The purchase of the new house was part of the plan that she and her husband prepared a few years before her retirement. As you might expect from an E-Type 2: The Enchanter, there are some aspects of her job that she misses. "I liked being the 'go-to' person and solving problems. I miss the mentoring and interacting with a purpose. I just miss being with and helping so many people every day." She has joined a tennis club and enjoys entertaining and spending time with family and friends. These activities have helped her to replace the valuable relationships with others that were so important to her during her working years.

When asked what recommendations she has for someone preparing for retirement, she said, "Never listen to anyone who tells you when to retire. No one knows the right time better than you do." She also believes that it is essential to have a plan and not just blindly wander into retirement without thinking about the life you want to live. "It helps to be happily married. It is important to have someone to be with during this stage of life."

As for the future, she is beginning to get the urge to become more active in her church and community, "I feel an obligation to do valuable things." When I asked if she was happy in this current period of her life, she gave it a rating of 90 percent "happy," 10 percent "not happy."

Now go to chapter 4.

ACTIVITY MAP

E-Type 3: The Star

The Star focuses on personal performance and strives to be successful.

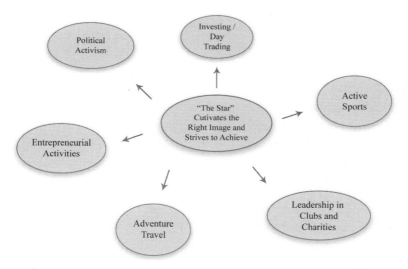

All of the Enneagram types can experience adjustment problems in retirement primarily due to their level of performance addiction; however, some of the types, just by their intrinsic nature, may be at higher risk for psychological disruption. As an E-Type 3: The Star, you have a high risk for experiencing emotional distress during the early and middle stages of retirement because of your constant need for achievement and general lack of self-awareness. Whenever The Star enters an environment that is not fast moving, action packed and achievement oriented, anxiety will be experienced.

You would be helped by involvement in religious, spiritual, and therapeutic programs where your "mask" or projected image is explored. A "step down" process should be considered, whereby you slowly ease into retirement whenever possible. Activities where you play a very active leadership role are most beneficial for you. More than anything you need to feel like a winner.

The Story of E

I first met E while he was the CEO and founder of a rapidly growing and highly successful one-hundred-employee health care-consulting firm. I found E to be intelligent, talented, and totally dedicated to the success of his firm. As an E-Type 3: The Star, he had always been successful. In high school he was the president of his class for four straight years. As a sales executive for a large medical device company, he consistently ranked at the very top of performers. When he was promoted to general manager at the medical device company, his track record of excellence continued; he racked up stellar achievement awards and received positive recognition.

A few years after our meeting, he sold his consulting firm to an investor group and became the president of the holding company. About twelve months later, he became embroiled in a conflict with the chairman and was abruptly terminated. He was forced to walk away from the firm he had created and sever the personal relationships he had established during the decade since the firm's founding. He was forced into retirement without any time to plan a transition to a new life. He was caught without options because it was inconceivable to him that he would not be successful in his new executive position. Although financially independent, he was only forty-eight years of age.

E's immediate emotional response was severe. As he reported, "I felt that I lost my identity. I had no idea what to do next. I felt as if I had been eviscerated—that I had a big hole in my chest. I withdrew and was in a funk—sometimes it felt hard to breathe." He recalls walking out of a Christmas party at his country club with emotional upset because he wanted to avoid discussing his termination. It was a terribly painful subject.

The first year after his sudden departure he maintained the rapid pace of his previous life through a frenetic variety of activities. He met with investment bankers several times a week. When he found this unsatisfying he switched to golf, which he played several times a week. After discovering that he would never be able to meet his high expectations of playing par golf, he dedicated himself to a strenuous exercise routine. Once again, this activity did not provide the satisfaction he sought. He could not find activities like those that had challenged and rewarded him during his working career. His anxiety and depression continued and came in waves—there was little relief.

During this period of time he became active with an investment group that he had known for several years and made a sizable investment in a firm that manufactured home fragrance. This turned out to be a mistake. As he comments, "I should not have made this investment. I knew nothing about this industry—I was just looking for something to do. I did not have the emotional equilibrium to make good decisions during this period."

E began making choices about what to do next. He made several important decisions. He resolved to relax more, do nothing for money, and oversee a major renovation to his eighteenth-century farmhouse, a project close to his heart. He also ran for local political office and served out a six-year term. Although these tasks brought great feelings of personal accomplishment and contribution, he still felt as though something was missing—he needed a different type of challenge.

Finally, after a great deal of experimentation and research, he made the decision to slowly and incrementally start another consulting business. The initial stages of this business offered exciting possibilities for introducing innovative marketing services to the health care industry. E stated, "I needed to create my own identity—reinvent myself. It was like I was on a journey to find what I really liked to do. I know I need to make an impact and have an intellectual challenge to be happy. I also need meaning in the things I do. I like to create value for others."

When I asked E what advice he would give a person planning for retirement, he felt that the person should make no major decisions shortly after retiring and should take the time to settle in and explore different options for his or her new life. He explained:

During this period you should re-center yourself to establish a strong emotional and physical foundation for new endeavors. You should explore different ideas of interest while making no significant decisions—financial or personal. Get back in touch with your spouse, your family, and your friends. It is a great time to work on yourself and to address all those things you put off for so long. Try to adopt a low-stress and healthier lifestyle—work on self-improvement.

When I asked if he was happy in this current period of his life, he gave it a 70 percent "happy," 30 percent "not happy" rating, but qualified this assessment by saying "My current happiness rating could just be a projection of my own demanding personality. I always think I could do better."

Now go to chapter 4.

ACTIVITY MAP

E-Type 4: The Drama Queen

The Drama Queen is artistic by nature and experiences life through high drama.

All of the Enneagram types can experience adjustment problems in retirement primarily due to their level of performance addiction; however, some of the types, just by their intrinsic nature, may be at higher risk for psychological disruption. As an E-Type 4: The Drama Queen, you have only a moderate risk for experiencing emotional distress during the early and middle stages of retirement. This is primarily because of your sensitive nature. You, more than any other type, have struggled to maintain your happiness for most of your life. Yes, you can be melodramatic, self-absorbed, and extremely needy; however, you have been forced to explore psychology, religion, and spiritual activities in order to make sense and order out of your life. More than anything you need greater hopefulness and faith.

Now go to chapter 4.

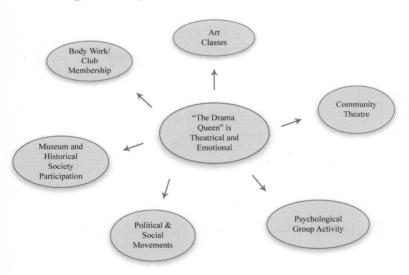

ACTIVITY MAP

E-Type 5: The Solitary Mystic

The Solitary Mystic is detached and independent and excels in the pursuit of special knowledge.

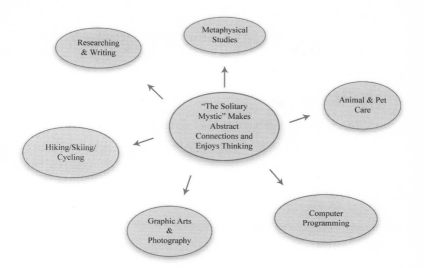

All of the Enneagram types can experience adjustment problems in retirement primarily due to their level of performance addiction; however, some of the types, just by their intrinsic nature, may be at higher risk for psychological disruption. As an E-Type 5: The Solitary Mystic, you have only a moderate risk for experiencing emotional distress during the early and middle stages of retirement. This temperate risk is primarily due to the "lone wolf" nature of this type. You can be happy being alone, close to nature, and without a lot of material things. You have learned to withdraw from your nurturing environment at an early age and limit your dependency on others. As a consequence you have been "driven into your head" and use your imagination and overactive thought processes as an escape from erratic and sometimes painful early circumstances. Retirement may likely be viewed more as a relief from outside pressures than a painful life transition. For you there is so much to think about and so little time. More than anything you need autonomy.

The Story of P

P was born into a blue-collar family. His father was a construction worker like most of the men in the town where he grew up. P cannot recall his father ever showing outward affection or playing with him during his early years. He did not think this was unusual because most fathers of this era did not seem to participate in childrearing. His mother was loving but was not the affectionate type. He recalls her as being very efficient and eternally busy. "I always had been cared for extremely well from a maintenance perspective, but not emotionally. My mother had a difficult life with few conveniences. Everything she did, however, was done well, such as cooking, cleaning, ironing, and being a supportive wife. She did not have much time for me because she was always busy taking care of others and work-ing around the house."

As P entered school he was only a fair student. He later learned that he suffered from attention defi-cit disorder, although it was not diagnosed at the time. He won an athletic scholarship to college and encountered the usual life adjustments associated with leaving home for the first time. He reports that he knew at an early age that he had to make it on his own. "There was no safety net there for me."

As P matured he became more and more academically inclined. He graduated with a decent grade point average and started his first job. From that point on in his life, he became a high achiever. He was considered a rising star in every organization where he was employed. He acquired graduate degrees and then started his own company. He worked continuously and alone. He had no partners or others to help carry the load. As he said, "These were difficult years."

He began to notice several personality characteristics about himself that concerned him, such as his need to be alone to recharge his batteries, his dislike of social events, his resistance to others who attempted to make claims on his time and energy, and his passion for solitary hobbies such as reading and computers. He also realized that he had created a public persona that did not resemble his true self. Being an E-Type 5: The Solitary Mystic he was forced to function in public in a way that betrayed his gut instincts. "I knew what it took to be successful—what other people expected of someone like me, and I became good at it, but it wore me down and sapped my spirit even though I was successful."

After many years, P sold his company and retired to a small town in a rural area near his hometown. In true E-Type 5 fashion, he enjoyed the solitude and privacy afforded by his location. After a year he began to feel increasing anxiety and emotional pressure. "I thought retirement for me would be easy. But I cut myself off from other people to such an extent that I had almost no social life or involvement with others except my immediate family. I felt no interest or attraction for anything. Normally solitude would not be a problem for me for short periods, but this felt more like exile."

P was used to leading a very active life full of challenges and new experiences. "I felt really lousy and I knew there was something wrong. I seemed to be irritated and angry all the time." When I asked him how he resolved his emotional stress he indicated that he began searching for activities that gave him pleasure and became committed to projects that brought him into closer contact with a few friends and former business associates. "I learned that there are only a few things I am really interested in, such as making money, travel, movies, computers, and books." When I asked him what recommendations he would give to those entering retirement he said, "Stay true to yourself, don't try to become someone you're not. Accept the fact that retirement may not be as easy as you might think—an adjustment will be required. Be experimental and be confident that you will find your way out of the wilderness, but you must be smart about it." Today P gives himself a happiness rating of 75 percent "happy," and 25 percent "unhappy."

Now go to chapter 4.

ACTIVITY MAP

E-Type 6: The Closet Rebel

The Closet Rebel is dutiful and loyal and is attracted to strong leaders and underdog causes.

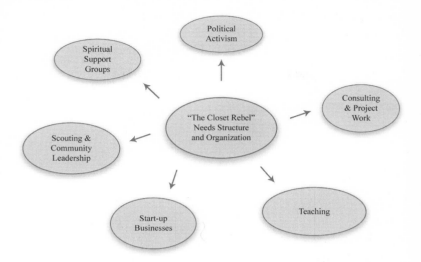

All of the Enneagram types can experience adjustment problems in retirement primarily due to their level of performance addiction; however, some of the types, just by their intrinsic nature, may be at higher risk for psychological disruption. As an E- Type 6: The Closet Rebel, you have only a modest risk for experiencing emotional distress during the early and middle stages of retirement. This low-risk profile is primarily due to your cautious and inhibited nature. You sense danger around every corner and therefore follow established rules and regulations, provided they increase your feelings of security. You can align yourself to movements and causes that have a strong appeal. You fit in well with organizations that require hierarchy and orderly processes. You are seldom flamboyant but are attracted to self-assured leaders. More than anything you need structure and increased feelings of safety and security.

Now go to chapter 4.

ACTIVITY MAP

E-Type 7: The Cruise Director

The Cruise Director is charming and cheerful with a positive self-image.

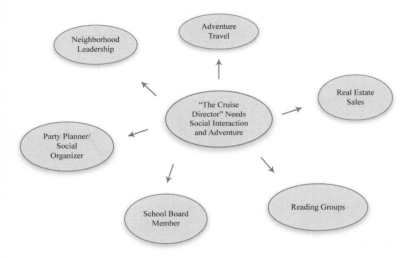

All of the Enneagram types can experience adjustment problems in retirement primarily due to their level of performance addiction; however, some of the types, just by their intrinsic nature, may be at higher risk for psychological disruption. As an E-Type 7: The Cruise Director, you have only a moderate risk of experiencing emotional distress during the early and middle stages of retirement. This is primarily due to your positive, action-oriented, and other-directed orientation. As long as you remain socially engaged, pursue your interests, and have fun things to plan and look forward to, there is little likelihood of serious emotional disturbance during retirement. Most of all you need admiration and attention.

Now go to chapter 4.

ACTIVITY MAP

E-Type 8: The Conquistador

The Conquistador likes to take charge and exert power and control over those who are in the position to influence his or her life.

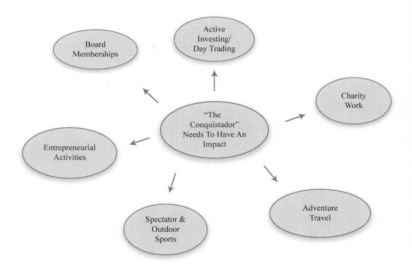

All of the Enneagram types can experience adjustment problems in retirement primarily due to their level of performance addiction; however, some of the types, just by their intrinsic nature, may be at higher risk for psychological disruption. As an E-Type 8: The Conquistador, you have a very high risk of experiencing emotional distress during the early and middle stages of retirement. This is primarily due to your competitive and aggressive nature. In addition, you can become easily bored and will take excessive risks to stimulate the action you need to attain emotional equilibrium. You possess a lethal combination of high energy, and the need for action and a large playing field—seldom available during retirement. You need to make certain that you have pre-established projects and interests in which to channel your energy after retirement. In addition, you could benefit from spiritual and psychological investigations that bring you in touch with the driving forces behind your personality. Introspection may be a rather new and threatening process for you, and one you may resist. More than any other type, you require the greatest psychological reconciliation between your innermost instincts and the dynamics of your living environment postretirement. More than anything you need the truth.

The Story of K

K retired at the age of forty-eight after being the president and COO of two of the largest retailers in the country. He would not be in favor of using the term "retirement" to describe his transition; it was more of a readjustment to an active but less frenetic lifestyle. He admits that he was finished with the constant pressures of corporate life and looked forward to charting a new course. He had achieved financial independence and was able to pursue personal interests and provide assistance to others by sitting on several boards and funding a charity.

K is an E-Type 8: The Conquistador and therefore had focused his ample energy and stamina on his career to the exclusion of most other activities. He considered his career the most important thing in his life other than his family. He liked having the power and resources to make a positive impact and achieve goals and objectives. Most importantly, he was attracted to the action, pace, and complexity of corporate life. He felt a total immersion in the discussions and thinking processes required for success. He would describe it as the freedom of involvement based on thinking quality—to move in and out of issues and discussions and accelerate things forward.

When K retired he took three months off and then gave himself six additional months to define the next stage of his life. He managed this transition very well and secured both investment relationships and board seats, which were both part of his original plan.

It was not until two or three years after his retirement that he began to feel psychological discomfort. As he would describe it, "After a while the loss of intensity got to me. There were gaps or downtime where I had nothing to think about and that made me feel valueless and depressed. The pain was on the same level as when my father died." He was mourning the loss of his engagement in intense action and large and complex issues at any time of his choosing. Feeling out of balance he states that his attempts at introspection only made the pain worse. The greatest benefit he received at this critical time was lengthy and repeated discussions with his spouse regarding his emotional distress. He states, "If you don't have a soul mate to talk with I recommend psychological counseling because an E-Type 8 needs to reduce the internal pressure or self-destructive behavior could result."

I asked K what recommendations he would offer those a few years away from retirement. He suggested to start thinking about what you like to do that makes you happy. Also he recommends slowing down and becoming more aware of yourself and the needs of your spouse. Determining the E-Type of your spouse could be an important step in managing your transition. Also he mentioned the importance of your geographical location as an essential ingredient of happiness—he calls it finding your spot.

Today K says that he is content about 80 percent of the time. He says, "The old longing for more action creeps in occasionally but I find great satisfaction from helping others from my board and charity work."

Now go to chapter 4.

ACTIVITY MAP

E-Type 9: The Harmonizer

The Harmonizer is quiet, relaxed, and noncompetitive, with a good sense of proportion and balance.

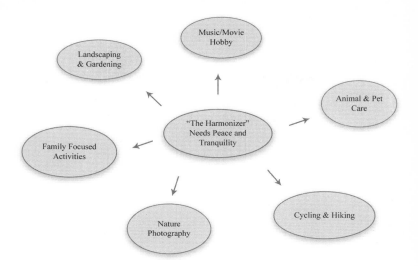

All of the Enneagram types can experience adjust-ment problems in retirement primarily due to their level of performance addiction; however, some of the types, just by their intrinsic nature, may be at higher risk for psychological disruption. E-Type 9: The Harmonizer has a very low risk of experiencing emotional distress during the early and middle stages of retirement. This is primarily due to your subdued and contented nature. You make very little demands upon your environment and are happy doing routine chores and enjoyable activities. More than any other type, you lack high energy and willpower and easily adapt to the needs of others. Because of your well-bal-anced and stable characteristics, you may experience retirement as the happiest time of your life. More than anything you need peace.

Now go to chapter 4.

Chapter 4

Happiness Realizations

While adjusting to retirement, I found it necessary to also investigate my spiritual beliefs, which were central to how I viewed life in general. I launched this investigation because I suspected that I had never completely adopted a core set of spiritual beliefs and consequently they were not definitive enough to provide sufficient emotional support during my rocky transition to retirement. I could also hear the clock ticking and felt a growing sense of urgency to make some hard-core decisions regarding how the "unseen" world operates. I had put this task off for as long as possible because I had always resisted making a commitment to any definitive set of principles. As you will learn, I have not been exactly a poster child for living the straight and narrow when it comes to formal religion. You might say I discovered a few holes that needed filling before I could feel any confidence that my beliefs could withstand the ultimate test of life, which in my case was retirement.

Growing up I was what you might call a spiritual vagabond. I was raised a Presbyterian by my parents but my commitment lapsed during college. I always held a rather ill-informed and hazy view of formal religion, but held fast to basic core beliefs, such as the Ten Commandments, and tried to live by them as best I could. I attempted to reactivate my commitment to organized religion after college but it just didn't stick. I felt as though something was missing—that there was more to the story.

In my thirties and forties I became attracted to Buddhism. I spent a great deal of time pondering the religion's tenants and investigated its ancient texts and modern interpretations. I became a philosophical Buddhist, meaning that I integrated its wisdom into my life and discovered that it did not conflict with my other spiritual views. The Noble Eightfold Path and the Four Noble Truths represent a great spiritual contribution to the world.

A secular view did not make sense to me because I felt that it granted divine powers to the human ego—that whatever you believed was backed by universal truth. I did not believe that my puny self had sufficient knowledge or clarity of understanding of universal spiritual laws for me to call my own shots regarding how to live. Also it seemed to reject the divine power of Jesus Christ, Buddha, and Krishna, who continue to influence the entire world simply on the basis of their earthly sojourn. These three avatars possessed extraordinary knowledge and immense personal power. Their truth was a pure and direct transmission of divine energy that continues to reverberate throughout the world. Their power was projected through the extremely high frequency of their consciousness. As we have learned from electrical power transmission, the higher the frequency the greater the power. Consequently, the conscious energy of these holy figures echoes with unimaginable power even to this day. If you would like to verify this statement, try this. The next time you see a fisherman, walk up to him and say, "Follow me." See what happens. Unless you're Jesus gathering his disciples, I guarantee you he is not going to throw his fishing pole into the water and get in your car.

During my fifties and early sixties, I guess you could have called me a Christian/Buddhist. At the time, I still had the uneasiness of knowing I had not committed to any individualized or specific religion, but had instead adopted a set of beliefs that resembled something you would order off of a menu in a Chinese restaurant. But my faith never wavered and I never stopped searching. I subjected myself to every possible spiritual teaching, including those some might consider controversial, such as the "Seth" books and *A Course in Miracles*.

As I mentioned, during my search for better psychological equilibrium I decided that I needed more than greater self-understanding. The Enneagram identified limitations of my personality that I wanted to do something about. I wanted to transform myself so that I could become free of the restrictions presented by my personality type. These restrictions were limiting my freedom and were causing many of the frustrations

I experienced during my transition to retirement. I also decided that I needed a more expansive spiritual worldview from which to guide my growth and understanding. Increased psychological awareness represented knowledge of the inner self; I also needed a new set of spiritual guideposts to guide my outward actions in the future. I once again found the answer within the Enneagram, in what Almaas calls "Holy Ideas." Holy Ideas offer a very enlightened and unified view of reality. They presented me with a course of action that I began to follow. Over time, my satisfaction and contentment began to grow. I discovered that when I align my thinking with sacred truths the inevitable result is greater peace and contentment.

What follows is an introduction to a set of spiritual principles derived from the Enneagram that I believe transcend traditional religious doctrine. You will learn that many of these principles are receiving surprising support from current research in quantum physics. For example, I recently learned of a $1.42 million award being granted to an eighty-seven-year-old French physicist by the name of Bernard d'Espagnat. He was awarded the Templeton Prize, which honors a living person who has made an exceptional contribution to affirming life's spiritual dimension. How, you may ask, does a physicist win such a prize? He played a key role from the mid-sixties to the early eighties pioneering research in quantum physics, particularly studying Bell's Theorem. He said, "Those among our contemporaries who believe in a spiritual dimension of existence and live up to it are, when all is said, fully right." He, among others, has discovered that at the very foundation of matter—the building blocks of existence—lies a spiritual energy that can be observed and measured.

It is my hope that the understanding and adoption of the principles that follow into your everyday life will make your psychological transition to retirement a much easier task. These principles are directly related to your E-Type and will help you to assuage specific propensities you may have that could cause you problems. I call these "Happiness Realizations" because as you contemplate and integrate these principles into your everyday life, your emotional stress will be reduced and your sense of peace and happiness will increase—I can personally attest that this is true.

Linear Versus Nonlinear Reality

Have you ever gone to the movies and watched a very inspiring and moving performance and then later, over coffee with a good friend, tried to describe how you felt about the movie? Most people struggle to find the right words to fully and accurately convey their feelings. They end up saying something trite such as "It was a really good movie." or "I thoroughly enjoyed it." or "I give it five stars." It seems futile and incomplete to put into concrete terms the strong emotional reaction you experienced. There is a fairly simple explanation for this phenomenon—watching a movie is a nonlinear experience, not easily analyzed and converted in linear or discrete terms. As you read on you will learn why this happens and what it means.

The spiritual realm is nonlinear by nature, whereas our conventional world is lived in a linear fashion. Many people believe the linear world is the only reality that exists. Things you can analyze and measure characterize this environment. It is tangible and functions in accordance with scientific laws. In school you learned chemistry, math, and science so that you could manipulate and control this world. The U.S. is one of the most scientifically minded countries in the world; in fact our entire society is built upon the scientific method. The people who seem to get ahead in this linear world are those that can manipulate its symbols with the greatest proficiency. Icons of industry such as Henry Ford, Andrew Carnegie, and Thomas Edison were masters of this realm.

The strength of our self-identity largely depends upon how well we navigate the ebb and flow of this physical setting. Achievement addicts have shown themselves to be particularly skilled at functioning in this environment for the benefit of themselves and their organizations. The person whose scholarship best characterizes this linear world is Sir Isaac Newton, the English physicist who introduced civilization to the idea that nature operates in an orderly fashion, being both predictable and controllable. His was a major contributor to the scientific thinking of his day and his scientific principles remain the basis of modern society. However, recent discoveries in quantum physics have challenged several of his underlying assumptions about how the world really works.

In addition to the linear reality that we perceive and live within, there is another reality that is slightly more difficult to grasp and understand—this is non-linear reality. This type of reality does not function in accordance with a set of mathematical rules—it is the world of dreams, meaningful coincidences, feelings, emotions, and new ideas. Nonlinear reality can be mysterious and confusing; it also can be very threatening to those of us who have mastered the linear mode of thinking. In fact, by many of those operating solely from the Newtonian paradigm, it is misunderstood or completely ignored; it seems to be too uncontrollable and contradictory to take seriously. There have been societies that have operated comfortably in this nonlinear reality, such as Tibetan Buddhists, Native American Indians, Australian Aborigines, (who date back over 50,000 years), and, of course, those working at Apple (only kidding). If you have traveled to India you can feel the Hindu influence everywhere, which is a very spiritual type of nonlinear energy.

What makes the nonlinear domain so challenging is that it is so elusive; its affects are emitted but never secured. While linear reality is anchored in time, nonlinear reality is not fixed in time, but affixed to consciousness. It doesn't operate by the same set of rules as the linear domain because it defies measurement; it is much more subtle and nondescript. It is nearly impossible to analyze and even more challenging to grasp. Instead of certainty, it functions on probability. A nonlinear action is initiated based on belief rather than evidence. Our material world operates in tandem with the nonlinear; however, our modern scientific society functions mostly in linear mode and treats nonlinear influences as error variance that must be controlled. It operates under the mantra "If you can't measure it how can you be sure that it exists?" A nonlinear breakthrough has the power to change the world; a linear breakthrough has the power to change a process. The intellect is not the highest order manifestation of man, consciousness is.

Power moves from the linear to the nonlinear. When linear thinking is taken to the extreme, you get the computer models that guided Wall Street into making catastrophic investment decisions and created the nuclear bomb. When in linear mode you make decisions based on the data; when in nonlinear mode you make decisions based on the heart. It may be somewhat of a shock, but the future of our country depends upon how well we navigate this nonlinear realm because it is the source of all new ideas and innovations, the lifeblood of our economy.

It is interesting to note that some of the most significant economic advances of recent years have been the result of the coalescence of nonlinear extrapolations (innovations) from existing technologies; the iPhone and iPod are excellent examples of this. From a monetary perspective, innovation and design are much more powerful than rule-governed thinking alone. This is, in part, because of the immense technological and social impact of these highly creative conceptual leaps.

Linear thinking has built the modern world that we all know and love, but it is not all-powerful. It has the ability to make us money but not make us happy. The older we get the more this becomes evident in our lives. In his best-selling book *A Whole New Mind: Why Right-Brainers Will Rule the Future*, Daniel Pink states that baby boomers are losing interest in pursuing wealth and are now in search of meaning in their lives. He calls meaning the "new money." "Meaning," of course, is a nonlinear concept that resists appraisal and close examination—it is a judgment or interpretation. You know meaning when you feel it.

What functions are nonlinear in our world? There are music, literature, art, theatre, and design. Of course, religion and any type of spiritual practice such as meditation, prayer, and contemplation are attempts by us to open a channel to this domain. Intuition and human emotions may also be considered nonlinear because they are nonquantifiable. Overall, creativity is fundamentally a nonlinear process. You cannot mandate that someone be creative, you can only encourage or cajole it into existence.

> "When a thing is new, people say: 'It is not true.'
> Later, when its truth becomes obvious, they say: 'It's not important.'
> Finally, when its importance cannot be denied, they say 'Anyway, it's not new.'"
>
> —William James

It is interesting to note that the most important nonlinear aspect of ourselves is our soul, or spiritual essence. We usually think of ourselves in linear terms because of the workings of our bodies, but what about our spirit, intuitions, emotions, and dreams? If, under hypnosis, you cracked open our subconscious I can guarantee you that rabbits are not going to jump out of our skulls. You are going to unleash a crazy quilt of feelings and emotionally charged associations—all nonlinear stuff. So deep inside all of us is a connection to this nonlinear realm. But the modern world has weakened our bond to it through an overreliance on science and measurement as the principle explanations of our reality.

Throughout history there have been sages or masters who made contact with and explored this nonlinear realm. Just as there are adepts at mathematics and music, there are individuals who could be considered spiritual adepts—individuals who have elevated their spiritual knowledge and ability to the absolute extreme. There is a common consensus among these individuals that the nonlinear world is composed of spiritual energy. We always hear stories about the monk in the attic or the ascetic meditating in a cave and we laugh because it seems so outrageous to us that anyone would ever want to live their life like that. Of course, that is a linear assessment of a nonlinear process. We don't know what the monk in the attic or the ascetic meditating in a cave are experiencing. We don't know their realizations or wisdom, only their seeming eccentricity.

Almost any direct experience of divine energy would cause us to challenge our understanding of reality. I have an acquaintance that told me that he went to see the Dalai Lama and walked into the room and burst into tears for no apparent reason. I know of another person who was awakened in the middle of the night feeling love so intensely she thought she was having a heart attack. I could list many reported experiences like this. How do we explain these experiences? Should they be dismissed as craziness or did these individuals somehow come into contact with some divine form of energy?

It is also worthy to note that those societies who function in accordance with the nonlinear domain are the most spiritual and peaceful. Tibet was one of the most highly evolved countries in the world, totally unprepared for China's invasion. One might say that they were a backward culture, unprepared to function in the modern world. It appears that the exact opposite is closer to the truth. Tibetans evolved to a level where they were vulnerable to invasion because their world-view was based on compassion—the core teaching of Buddhism—and consequently had no standing army or sophisticated weapons to use for their defense.

A comparable analogy would be a priest getting into a street brawl with a gang member over the fact that the father wore a black suit. The priest most likely would lose the fight but who is more aligned with truth, more capable of compassion, more resilient in the face of challenge? Peacefulness is the result of living a life that is guided by spiritual awareness of the invisible realms of existence. The higher the spiritual evolution of a culture, the more peaceful and happy are its people. As we grow as human beings, we move from the linear toward the nonlinear, from analysis to intuition, from desire to more meaningful aspirations.

As we progress through our retirement transition, it is important to remember that nonlinear reality is what makes us uniquely human. Living in accordance with divine energy makes us happy; living in disharmony with it makes us unhappy because our lives are under the control of a tyrant—our ego. The consensus view of reality accepted by the modern world as gospel cannot possibly support our happiness. Have you ever felt that true happiness is elusive, even though you have every possible material thing you ever wanted or needed? Have you spent much of your life seeking diversions from restlessness and dissatisfaction? The reality is that the ego has created an artificial life so radical that it has moved us away from our true identity, which is to live in complete harmony with divine energy. This is a fundamental truth.

As I mentioned earlier, all E-Types have endured a breach of trust to some extent through their early nurturing environment. Because of this separation, our connection with divine energy was slightly weakened or severely limited. This reaction to our early environment led to judgment errors that have been a source of our suffering to this day. For example, The Masters feel that there is something inherently wrong with them and that they need to strive for perfection; The Enchanters feel a sense of separation and that they can't have their own way; The Stars feel unsupported and take matters into their own hands; The Drama Queens feel disconnected and need control; The Solitary Mystics feel separate from everything; The Closet Rebels feel a sense of distrust and cynicism;

The Cruise Directors feel they can direct their own life even though something feels lacking; The Conquistadors feel a sense of self-blame and anger; and The Harmonizers feel inferior and flawed.

Deep in the core of our personalities these beliefs exist. They were put there by genetic predisposition and resulted from our attempts to avoid discomfort and pain. They were used as a defense against a perceived lack of care and attention. These may be very moderate inclinations or rather severe tendencies, depending on the quality of our early nurturing environment. We are going to address each of these false beliefs later in this chapter with our nine Happiness Realizations. Now let's learn about the laws of divine energy and how we can start using them to improve our life as we transition into retirement.

Divine Energy

While we are basically a spirit inhabiting a body, we became a body devoid of spirit when our trust faltered as children and our ego became preeminent. It is easy to understand why our lives are lacking in spiritual understanding. We can taste and touch the physical world but we can't see the spiritual world around us; it is nonlinear. There is

> "There is an unseen order, and to that our supreme good lies in harmoniously adjusting ourselves hereto."
>
> —William James, *The Varieties of Religious Experience: A Study in Human Nature*

a price to be paid for this omission. Our perception is of a physical world that is highly competitive, randomly dangerous, and mostly unsupportive, providing only the comfort we glean for ourselves through sustained efforts. We are alone in this world and we know it. We lost our trust when we lost touch with the loving nature of divine energy, which offers us goodness, perfection, and meaning. As long as you cannot perceive this truth, you will never be able to reconnect with your divine nature and you will feel alone and abandoned.

> "In order to know yourself, you must understand the universe, and to know the universe, you must understand yourself."
>
> —Arnold Mindell, PhD, *Quantum Mind: The Edge Between Physics and Psychology*

Now let me say it for you, "What kind of new age bullshit is this?" For you to accept the sustained presence of divine energy may cause your ego to overreact. This is understandable because your ego is not your partner—it is the boss. It does not share, it controls. It is a dictator that tells you how things are going to be. This is not how it was supposed to be—you were not designed to have an ego with dominion over your life. Think of it as an interloper that snatched control when you were young and helpless. The more we feel supported by the universe, the more we can relax and feel confident regarding our place in the world. Whereas, the more control we grant the ego the more conflict and frustration we introduce into our life.

After I retired and began experiencing psychological discomfort, I made the decision to do everything I could to learn more about the field of divine energy. I suspected that my personal growth and happiness depended upon how well I understood and related to this spiritual realm of influence. Often this energy is called God, but I use the terms "divine energy," "divine field," and "divine spirit" in this book because they offer a broadly spiritual, rather than a religious, connotation.

I encountered serious internal resistance and found it actually absurd to think that this loving energy was everywhere, in everything, and active. I thought, "Where have you been all my life?" Then I looked back and recalled an automobile accident I'd had in college after having one too many. Over several beers, I'd listened to my college roommate pine away for his lost girlfriend. After leaving the bar, we got in his car and hit a tree head-on going fifty-five miles per hour at one o'clock in the morning. As I saw the tree coming, with no seat belt on, I put my arms up to protect my head, which was about to crash into the windshield. In a split second my arms were perfectly placed against the glass; when my head struck my arms, they dispersed the force of the impact and my head did not break the windshield. My roommate's leg hit the floor-mounted gearshift so hard it bent it back against the dashboard. When I exited the car after the crash I felt severe pain in my arms but they were not broken. In fact, after about ten minutes they felt normal. My roommate exited the car with no broken bones. To this day I don't know how we did not get killed or seriously injured in the crash. Was I alone or was divine energy supporting me on that crazy night? Do you have a similar story?

I find that grasping the notion or conceptualizing the truth that spiritual energy is available and capable of loving me, supporting me, and helping me extremely difficult. I have always adhered to the statement, "The truth works." By this I mean that if something is true then it consistently fulfills its function. If it is false, it will veer off course, or become erratic in some fashion. I always thought in concrete terms. My own willfulness seemed to be blocking me. Therefore, I put myself through a test of sorts. If divine energy is truth, I should not have to work at it or take responsibility for it—I should just open the channel and let it enter. I began acting as if divine energy was around me at all times, even if I had trouble believing it.

I converted the postulates Almaas calls Holy Ideas into nine simple statements, each one associated with an Enneagram type. I reviewed these statements once or twice daily for no more than two or three minutes. I found support for this approach from Dr. Hawkins who states in *Transcending the Levels of Consciousness*, "From nonlinear dynamics also emerges the principle of 'iteration' by which a repeated choice or option pro-gressively becomes a likelihood."[1] I named the nine statements "Happiness Realizations" because over time I began to actually feel more relaxed and more in touch with myself—the self I used to know fifty years ago. I

---

1. Hawkins, *Transcending the Levels of Consciousness*, 359.

began to sense a very subtle gentleness but also a feeling of release. I was only one small cell in the body of God, but not God himself. I was a passenger on his train; he was not a passenger on mine. As strange as it may seem, I felt unburdened by the acceptance of my own helplessness. I no longer had to carry the water. It all wasn't up to me. I could let go. I could do the unthinkable and slowly trust divine energy to support me and show me the way. The physicist Evan Harris Walker describes this process in *The Physics of Consciousness: The Quantum Mind and the Meaning of Life* when speaking of divine energy:

> This is a God of our collective will and the collective will of the universe. This is a God that has the potential of any knowledge that we know. A God that has the power to make any event occur and yet is restrained by the limits of our own minds. A God that pervades all things and yet acts through our vision.[2]

It is now a well-established fact that the act of observing things somehow affects the reality of what we observe. By directing our consciousness to anything, it alters the physical reality of what we observe. We are partners in creating the world that we see. Our attention activates a dance of consciousness, and we are full-fledged cohorts in creating the reality that we know, trust, and act upon. That means that there is scientific

---

2. Walker, *The Physics of Consciousness*, 336.

support for changing the reality that we experience by changing our beliefs about that reality, which leads us to the next section, Happiness Realizations.

Happiness Realizations

What follows are the nine Happiness Realizations, along with an explanation of each one. I would like you to review them, consider them, and listen to your inner voice. Try to assess how you feel while you read them. Do you sense resistance or do you have an inner sense of recognition that you are rediscovering deep truths long lost?

#1: Everything Is Perfect as It Is

First comes judgment then perception. If you make a judgment that something is imperfect, that is your reality—imperfection. How is it possible to be happy and relaxed when everything you see around you is flawed? It is torture. Standards require evaluations, which require judgments, which trigger your emotions. It is extremely easy to see imperfections; just set your standards extremely high then measure everything against them.

Consider what would happen if you began accepting rather than judging. You accept the beauty of a rose as being a perfect manifestation of that particular rose. You accept the beauty of your pet as being a perfect manifestation of that particular animal. And the big whopper, you accept yourself as the perfect manifestation of divine energy.

This Happiness Realization has particular resonance for The Master. At your core is the belief that there is something seriously wrong with you. This is a delusion that you have accepted as truth. When you feel flawed, you then begin to generalize these feelings of imperfection and project them onto other things. During your nurturing years you did not always feel you measured up to the standard being set—you were fundamentally flawed in some way. When, through comparison, you feel broken inside, you try to repair yourself through self-criticism, righteous indignation, and the rigid evaluation of others. You go on a compulsive campaign of judging, and bring perfection to everything within your reach. You feel that you can never rest until everything, including yourself, is perfect. As you well know, this brings on constant stress and unhappiness.

For this Happiness Realization to work its magic in your life, you need to accept that everything is composed of divine energy, and that this energy is flawless. You are made from this energy, as is everything else around you. If something is imperfect in your judgment, then you have not accepted the fact that "God don't make no junk." If you can release the notion of "wrongness" as being embedded deep in your very soul and

> "The universe is sacred.
> You cannot improve it.
> If you try to change it, you will ruin it.
> If you try to hold it you will lose it."
>
> —Lao-tzu, *Tao te Ching*

acknowledge the perfection and loving nature of the divine energy all around you, you will experience self-acceptance and liberation. It is impossible to overlook what you expect to see. If you expect to see imperfection, that is exactly what you will encounter; if you expect to see expressions of divine perfection, that is exactly what you will experience. All you need to do is stop comparative judgment for this to occur.

The lightness of being comes when you least expect it. It arrives on a silver steed of new awareness. Let go of your faulty old critical awareness and welcome in a new perception of light. There is nothing wrong with you, there never has been anything wrong with you, and there never will be anything wrong with you. Everything is perfect as it is.

#2: Going with the Flow Has Power

Divine energy is truth in operation. When you experience the truth, you feel a oneness or an interconnectedness operating in a harmonious flow with the universe. The truth unfolds based on specific laws of action. Lynne McTaggart describes it in her book *The Field: The Quest for the Secret Force of the Universe* as such:

> At our most elemental, we are not a chemical reaction, but an energetic charge. Human beings and all living things are a coalescence of [divine] energy in a field of energy connected to every other thing in the world. This pulsating

energy field is the central engine of our being and our consciousness, the alpha and the omega of our existence.[3]

Interaction with this divine energy field creates a flow or direction of force that operates in accordance with universal laws. Everything that occurs in this field is connected to everything else; there is no such thing as independent action. This field creates a direction and particular momentum and is based on infinite intelligence. Every event that unfolds in this field is optimal and an expression of divine will. Divine energy does not operate outside of perfection.

The best way to manage this divine energy flow is to move in accordance with it. That's why this Happiness Realization states that "going with the flow has power." You are, in effect, aligning your life with the flow of divine power rather than against it. Moving against this flow is an act of ignorance by the ego, which believes that it is God. This makes life difficult—things just don't seem to work out no matter how hard you try. If success does seem imminent, it inevitably collapses in failure and frustration.

When you place your will in accordance with divine energy, you feel a sense of release. This is experienced as a yielding and harmonization with the flow. You can always tell when you are in alignment because good things start occurring without great effort. Occasionally, phenomenal events arise that seem like

---

3. McTaggart, *The Field*, xiii.

miracles. When we fail in this effort it is usually because we want something to happen right away—we lose patience and try to take matters into our own hands. This is seldom a good course of action. We have no way of knowing the divine plan and are left with only one option, which is to place our faith in the infinite intelligence of divine power. Relinquishing your false beliefs of control can be frightening. It feels like a great leap into the heart of darkness because you must reorient your entire perspective to the non-linear, which causes fear and discomfort.

> "People were more likely to succeed if, instead of believing in a distinction between themselves and the world, and seeing individual people and things as isolated and divisible, they viewed everything as a connected continuum of interrelations."
>
> —Lynn McTaggart, *The Field: The Quest for the Secret Force of the Universe*

It is interesting that we think we have so much control over our lives. Of course, this is a total illusion. You cannot guarantee that you will wake up in the morning, that you will continue breathing, that you won't have a fatal illness, that you won't be involved in an accident on the way to the grocery store, or that something terrible won't happen to a loved one. The truth is that you have no control, but you like the illusion because the other option—to think that you have no shield against the random chaos of life—is terrifying. Your only alternative is noninterference, letting life unfold based on a divine energy pattern without trying to understand it, without judging it, and with no preferences for the outcome. Any time you are in phase with divine energy you gain happiness and strength; whenever you are out of phase you are left with frustration and weakness.

This Happiness Realization is particularly important for The Enchanter. When you operate as a separate self in an attempt to get your own way, you behave counter to divine flow. Any action that is based on pride or ego runs into obstacles. Stubbornness, an attempt to exercise your will to get your own way, results in anger and frustration. The basic truth is that you don't have the personal power to control everything that happens. It is essential for you to acknowledge that you are not the center of the universe and lose no power in relinquishing control to divine will. Total and complete freedom occurs whenever you desire whatever divine will delivers, because the product of divine will is always perfection based on infinite intelligence.

#3: Independent Action Is Not Possible

The real world operates in interconnected unity; there is no rigid separation or boundaries that exist. As Mihaly Csikszentmihalyi states in his classic book *Flow,* "When people try to achieve happiness on their own, without the support of a faith they usually seek to maximize pleasures...Wealth, power, and sex become the chief goals that give direction to their strivings. But the quality of life cannot be improved this way."[4]

---

4. Csikszentmihalyi, *Flow,* 8.

Life does not unfold in a vacuum and you are not an independent actor on the stage of life. You are constantly exchanging energy within a unified field of divine consciousness, both influencing and being influenced by this field. You are not separate but a part of it. This expresses the truth behind Happiness Realization #3: "Independent Action Is Not Possible."

> "You are not your gain; neither are you your loss. Gain and loss are external to you, things with which your eternal soul is not concerned. Do not waste even a moment on gains and losses when death is plucking your ears saying, 'Live! I am coming.'"
>
> —Wu Wei, *I Ching Wisdom: Guidance from the Book of Changes*

The product of your interaction with this divine energy field is the sensing of inner guidance, of your thoughts unfolding in a specific direction, flowing in a unique way, with a creative freshness. When you resonate in accordance with this energy field, you experience an authentic sense of purpose that results in feelings of contentment and happiness. When you are not synchronous with this field, your ego is in control, drawing you away from harmony. We have all lived like this for much too long and have paid a steep price for relinquishing our true identity.

This Happiness Realization holds special meaning for The Star. You hold the basic belief that achievement occurs on its own through individualized effort and in isolation from outside influences. Because of this, the burden you have carried has been heavy.

The truth is that you have never been the creator or initiator of action, but function within a participatory universe; it is impossible to separate yourself from its influences and effects. You cannot make up your own rules independent of this field because you do not have the personal power to do so. You are not, in essence, an individual contributor because the universe is unfolding harmoniously at every moment carrying you along with it. It is the activity of the ego to feel separate, which is not your true nature. The ego becomes threatened from anything that weakens its control. When you remove yourself from the creative flow of divine energy, you lose your grounding—you operate from your own limited and restricted center without the support of the actualized divine energy field. As Meister Eckhart said, "One must not always think so much about what one should do, but rather what one should be." A highly evolved person has successfully neutralized the ego—this is called enlightenment. If you gain the insight that your incessant striving is the result of deeply embedded feelings of helplessness and vulnerability, that your true identity is not based upon your constant exertion and accomplishments, that your unceasing efforts will not lead you to peace and happiness, you will evolve toward the light of truth about yourself.

#4: Accept Helplessness as a Basic Human Condition

This Happiness Realization requires you to surrender to whatever happens with the trust that everything is moving in the right direction. Of course, this can be quite difficult because we have spent most of our lives trying to free ourselves from feelings of helplessness. We struggle and sacrifice in order not to appear weak, but as we learned from *Star Trek,* "Resistance is futile." I learned this while I witnessed the death of my father. He suffered from Alzheimer's disease in the last years of his life. Over a four-year period I watched him die a slow death every day. It was not the life that he wanted or chose, but what could I do? I did not possess the personal power to cure him or slow the advance of his terrible disease. It was extremely painful to witness his deterioration. Finally I surrendered, I had no alternative—there were no other options available to me. I was in the uncomfortable position of being helpless. Millions of people experience similar situations every day, yet we go to extremes to ignore our fundamental helplessness because it makes us feel small and powerless.

Whenever trouble arises we immediately move to gain control of the situation. This is an act that gets executed at the master control center—the ego. It is also evidence of a lack of trust. While my father was suffering from Alzheimer's there were two options available to me: (1) hate God and dwell in bitterness and anger; or (2) trust in the idea that there is divine intelligence operating in the universe and accept the fact that I had no idea what was going on with my father, why he was experiencing this disease, and what was going to happen to him after his death. I chose the latter and felt deep sadness but a sense of reconciliation that somehow everything was progressing in accordance with some grand plan that I could not possibly comprehend.

Our only defense and comfort when encountering helplessness is the strength of our knowledge and connection with divine spirit. If this connection is strong we have faith that things are unfolding in a beneficial way even if we don't understand it, that some optimal outcome will occur even if we can't comprehend it, and that peace and love are the source of divine energy and will be experienced when the conditions are right.

This Happiness Realization has special meaning for The Drama Queen. You feel as though you are separate and unique from the rest of humanity—that you are an independent "I." You consider yourself an original—one of a kind—a special person with unique talents and aptitudes. This view separates you from the grounding strength and support of divine energy. It makes you feel disconnected and detached from power. Rather than understanding that your talents and abilities are expressions of divine unity, you have the mistaken

> "Individually we have to work to change the basic perspectives on which our feelings depend. We can only do so through training, by engaging in practice with the aim of gradually reorienting the way we perceive ourselves and others."
>
> —Dalai Lama, *How to Practice: The Way to a Meaningful Life*

belief that it is coming from your specialness. This is flawed logic. If you were a wave in the ocean, you would have a specific identity for only a moment until you were subsumed back into the sea. Even though you were a wave for a period, you were an expression of the sea the entire time; you were never a wave all by yourself.

By your very nature, you want control when control is not possible. You try to exercise control in order to rid yourself of feelings of alienation and separation. It would be most beneficial if you could reestablish your connection with divine energy by listening to yourself. Try to find moments during the day when you do or say things that would indicate that you see yourself as the sea and not the wave. Realize that the wave loses nothing by enfolding back into the sea—it relinquishes its individualized identity only to reappear as a wave elsewhere along the continuum, always remaining in harmony. As the wave appears and disappears, its formation is effortless and controlled by the grand laws of nature. It is fundamentally helpless to alter the course of its actions. It remains in synchronization with the movement and force of the entire sea and is part of a cosmic dance of energy.

#5: Everything Is Interconnected

Modern physics, and particularly the work of Werner Heisenberg, has revealed that the very building blocks of nature, subatomic particles, cannot be divided into independent segments. At the heart of matter, things have no meaning in isolation but only in their network of dynamic interrelationships. As Lynne McTaggart states in *The Intention Experiment: Using Your Thoughts to Change Your Life and the World*, "The universe [is] not a storehouse of static, separate objects, but a single organism of interconnected energy fields in a continuous state of becoming."[5] The reality that we experience is constantly changing and evolving through conscious awareness. We will learn in the next chapter how we have the capacity to influence the world around us through our intentions and focused thought processes.

Because of these interrelationships at the very core of nature, there is nowhere for us to hide or avoid the results of life events. This Happiness Realization, "Everything Is Interconnected," is the actual expression of the unity of existence. It is impossible to remove yourself from the divine energy field; it would be like trying to separate your nose from your face. Accepting this fact creates the realization that you are a part of this divine energy field and consequently supported by it in every way. Just like the wave is a part of the sea, an expression of "sea-ness," and not a discrete entity operating by separate laws of nature, so are you a part of the divine energy field. Therefore, if divine energy provides unity, perfection, infinite intelligence, and loving grace, we then may be assured that those very same properties are available to us as well. Seawater is the same whether it is in a wave state or not; it is always inclusive of the sea.

---

5. McTaggart, *The Intention Experiment*, xxiii.

People can obviously be different from one another but not separate from them. Your consciousness knows no boundaries, but your ego believes that you are a body and separate from the divine flow of the universe. This is a fundamental falsehood and leads to intense suffering through feelings of isolation and alienation.

> "It is evident that this notion of spirituality is consistent with the notion of the embodied mind...The central awareness in these spiritual moments is a profound sense of oneness with all, a sense of belonging to the universe as a whole."
>
> —Fritjof Capra, *The Hidden Connections: A Science for Sustainable Living*

This is a particularly important understanding for The Solitary Mystic. You believe that you can protect yourself by distancing yourself from the rest of the world. You learned early in life that you could not always trust your surroundings and decided to take a powder, vamoose, hasta mañana, and see you later alligator. Separating yourself as much as possible from your early environment seemed like a good idea at the time; it reduced your sense of helplessness and vulnerability, but your lack of trust prevented you from becoming a card-carrying member of the family of life. In order for you to withdraw you had to make the decision that you were not part of the loving family of man, but something small, weak, incomplete, and wanting. This caused a break or schism with the divine energy field, resulting in fear and mental anguish.

It is essential that you reconfigure your sense of self so that you see yourself as an extension of the divine energy field and not separate from it. You are its representative to the world, held up by it, moved along by it, protected by it, and loved by it. When you gain this insight you will feel a sense of peace and joy like never before. You cannot possibly feel alone when you function in harmony with divine grace. You provide an irreplaceable ingredient to the living presence of the universe. You are its emissary, and while discharging your duties, no permanent harm will come to you. Not now, not ever.

#6: Your Spirit Cannot Be Disconnected from Divine Energy

Have you heard of women's intuition? My wife uses it on me all the time and it is really annoying. In the face of a situation where all of the facts are signaling trouble ahead she will say something like, "Don't worry about it. It's going to be fine. It will all work out in the end, you'll see." Usually, my reaction is something like, "How can you say that given the circumstances? That is completely illogical." She goes away feeling completely relaxed and patient with the unfolding of events and I go away feeling frustrated because I want to take action immediately.

Of course, in the long run she is usually correct. She has a sixth sense for things. I think her connection to the divine energy field is stronger than mine; she has more faith that things will work out without intervention. I, on the other hand, can't stand waiting for things to happen. I want to make them happen. While I would consider myself a recovering junkie, she, as you may have guessed, has never suffered from achievement addiction.

My overriding observation during these conversations with my wife is that her woman's intuition is nothing more than her exercising her connection with divine energy. There is something that feels elusive about this field. It is gentle, subtle, and nuanced, yet ever-present. It is easy to ignore—to walk away from—because it doesn't grab your attention. You must be quiet and listen. This is why meditation, prayer, and solitude in nature have been conventional means for getting in touch with it. I realize that my wife does not turn her intuition on and off; that would be impossible. It is as much a part of her as the color of her eyes. It is just that she is more attuned to it than I am. It is like a beacon from a lighthouse far away: always on, always visible, and always trustworthy. Even if you can't feel it, you are never disconnected from divine energy. Like the lighthouse, its beacon shines forth no matter the weather. If you are not in touch with it, recognize it, or believe that it exists, it doesn't matter. The light shines forth because that is its intrinsic nature. You are the child of this field and, just as a mother never abandons her child, divine spirit will never abandon you, even if you reject it or lack faith in its power. Like gravity, you see its effects but not its essence. There is a perfect truth within your soul that is designed to recognize this energy field, to feel it, to reconcile with it, to live in accordance with it without stress or anxiety. This is knowledge of the heart rather than the mind. It is not possible for you to decouple from it; however, you can ignore it or reject it. Strong souls have faith in this energy field and ride upon its waves; weak souls do not and empower their egos.

This is a particular lesson for The Closet Rebel. You are a cynic at heart and believe that life is a struggle for survival. This is a reflection of your absence of faith. You are suspicious that others are motivated by selfishness, and if any goodness is found, it is thought to be used to gain advantage. The basis of your cynicism is a lack of faith in human nature. You also use your cynicism as a sword for protection. If you can debunk or question something and not fall victim to its allure, you feel a sense of safety and security. Because of your early nurturing environment, you have lost your sense that anyone is going to be there for you out of pure love. You lost the sense that there is something precious inside of you that is worthy of love. Instead, you witnessed inauthentic nurturance that did not adequately register with your intrinsic spirit. Hence you see the world as a dangerous place, lacking in essential benevolence. You have a sense of distrust that pervades your world. With your constant

> "A reality completely independent of the mind that conceives it, sees it, or feels it, is an impossibility."
>
> —B. Alan Wallace, *Choosing Reality: A Buddhist View of Physics and the Mind*

emphasis on what could go wrong, you appear defensive and skeptical to those close to you. This is because you do not share a core faith in the buoyant properties of the divine energy field.

It is essential that you establish trust and confidence with your inner nature. You need faith that you are worthy of love without having to earn it. You must resist giving up on yourself or the goodness of those around you. You have heard the old adage "seeing is believing"; in your case you must believe in order to see. If you expect to find goodness and faith in your world, that is exactly what you will discover. The truth of reality is much different than what you experience on a daily basis. The force of the divine energy field is based on absolute reliability and essential goodness. If you are successful in gaining a true insight into this realization, you will become transformed by its contact. You were made to function within its influence; its potential is not a force outside of yourself but within you. Not to acknowledge this fact is to reject your birthright.

#7: There Is Divine Intelligence Unfolding at All Times

Thousands of years ago the ancients made the observation that all of life was constantly changing. Seeds grew into large plants. Animals were born, suckled by their mothers, grew, and then passed on. They also noticed that human beings followed the same cycle of birth, growth, and death. They realized that life had no fixed points; its only constant was change. When something reaches its limits of growth, it changes to its opposite. Lao-tzu is credited with authoring a small book of sayings titled *Tao te Ching* that contains this ancient wisdom. He is thought to have lived during the time of Confucius; therefore the book's contents are extremely old. It is interesting to note that the Tao described by Lao-tzu closely resembles the properties of the divine energy field.

> If you open yourself to the Tao, you are at one with the Tao and you can embody it completely. If you open yourself to insight, you are at one with insight and you can use it completely. If you open yourself to loss, you are at one with loss and you can accept it completely. Open yourself to Tao, then trust your natural responses; and everything will fall into place.[6]

Of course, modern physicists use different language to describe how the world works. They see the entire universe as nothing but energy—more specifically as a wave of probability or potential—until it interacts with human consciousness. At that moment of observation, faster than the speed of light, the observable wave of energy snaps into physical reality and is measurable. It is indisputable that there is a clear and concrete connection between matter and consciousness. Without human observation, it seems that the

---

6. Lao-tzu, *Tao te Ching*, chap. 23.

entire universe would convert back into energy. Arthur Schopenhauer describes this quantum view of reality: "Every man takes the limits of his own field of vision for the limits of the world." It is clear that our worldview is mostly dependent upon our level of consciousness. As we observe the world around us, quantum waves of energy are collapsing into materiality. I know this may sound crazy, but we literally create our world through our consciousness. The world basically functions more like statistical probabilities than concrete events. What you see is what you get.

Consciousness also acts as the portal through which divine energy flows. It is akin to waves of sunlight radiating out into a frictionless void until they encounter an awakened consciousness that responds as a receptor. If you cannot observe the Tao it cannot observe you. If there are no receptors, potentiality cannot become an actuality. If the radio is not turned on you cannot hear the music. Alternatively, if you hear the music you gotta dance. If your receptors are open it means that your consciousness is tuned in to the right frequency and the party can begin.

Hopefully it is clear that change is constant because consciousness is constant; a dynamic network of interactions occurs all over the world, all the time. Within these interactions is the flow of divine energy. It enters us through our consciousness. The higher the level of our consciousness, the more vibrant and active the energy field operates within us. When you hear of certain people being "enlightened," it means that all of their circuits are open—they are getting a full dose of divine energy and experiencing periodic states of ecstasy and bliss. Dr. David Hawkins, in *Power vs. Force*, recalls his direct experience of the divine energy field as a young boy caught in a severe snowstorm with temperatures twenty degrees below zero while on his paper route. The wind, cold temperature, and snow were so severe he feared for his life. So he dug a little cave into a large snow bank to shield himself from the blistering wind. Here is his description:

> The shivering stopped and was replaced by delicious warmth...and then a state of peace beyond all description. This was accompanied by a suffusion of light and a Presence of infinite love, which had no beginning and no end, and which was indistinguishable from my own essence. I became oblivious of the physical body and surroundings as my awareness fused with this all-present illuminated state. The mind grew silent; all thought stopped. An infinite Presence was all that was or could be, and it was beyond time or description.[7]

As you observe the actualization of divine energy, you will notice that it reveals infinite intelligence and does not exhibit random or chaotic tendencies; it appears to be following a divine plan. It is moving its own way and possibly not one you would anticipate. If you can accept this as truth, it helps you to trust

---

7. Hawkins, *Power vs. Force*, 10.

that divine guidance is the natural state of the universe and not something you must struggle to provide for yourself. As you live moment to moment, a spontaneous unfolding occurs that guides your actions. If, however, you live according to your own plan, you negate the divine guidance available to you. It requires trusting that the universe will provide you with what you need, though possibly not with what you want.

As Matthew 6:28 reads, "And why are you troubled about clothing? See the flowers of the field, how they come up; they do no work, they make no thread." So the universe does not need formal structure. It evolves spontaneously each moment in accordance with its own divine laws. Living with grace means that you trust that you are not being left out of the grand divine plan, that your evolution is part of the grand evolution of the universe, and that your retirement is a natural part of life's inevitable transformation.

This is a specific message for The Cruise Director. You believe that you can design and live according to your own plan, that the actions of your life are best left up to you. This blocks you from the all-inclusive unfolding brought forth by the flow of divine energy. Deep inside of you is a sense that you don't really know what to do, aren't sure which way to go, so it feels safe to live according to your own plan. If you are successful in gaining the realization that your full potential can best be realized by alignment with the divine plan of the universe, you will begin to relax and find peace. If you cannot achieve this realization you are relinquishing your power and turning your life over to your ego to direct and control events. It is a delusion that you know what should be happening next. When you relax into the moment with faith and trust, you become the expression of the divine energy field to the world.

#8: There Is Nothing to Be Obtained

If we were truly enlightened beings we would possess enormous personal power. This power would be gained by our deep realization that there is no passageway to follow, no illumination to attain, and no system to use. We would grasp the unity of the universe and live with the realization that everything is transpiring as it should—with perfection. All of existence expresses that perfection at every moment. Most importantly, we would know that there is nothing to be obtained, nothing to strive for. We already have everything we could ever possibly need. We would be at peace and feel contented. We would also be enormously powerful. Our power would come from our knowledge and insight about how things really are in the world. It would be the power of liberation, the understanding that every-thing is complete at every moment and it is not our responsibility to change anything, do anything, or be anywhere other than where we are at that moment. This requires the acceptance that perfection exists at all times because there is nothing that needs to be done, no action to be taken, and nothing to be obtained. Life simply manifests moment to moment in perfection.

Few of us live like this because we've lost our grasp on the truth that beauty just is and we just are.

Nothing needs to be done for our perfection to manifest, just relaxation into each moment. What a gift we have been given. Even in the experience of suffering nothing must be done about it. It is a reality for that moment and then it is given up to the divine. This is not a passive stance toward life, but the placement of the responsibility and authority where it belongs—bathed in a divine energy solution. Reality is an expression that cannot be anything else but perfect. If some action needs to be taken, it will materialize and become self evident without struggle or doubt.

What makes this idea so difficult to grasp? Deep inside of us there is a feeling of guilt. From a Christian perspective, we were ejected from paradise because of our own willful choices, not those of God. As we look further, we discover this sense of guilt arose because we abandoned what was real inside of us, and we blame ourselves. In *Facets of Unity*, Almaas speaks of it as abandonment:

> Here you see that you have carried within you a profound sense of guilt for losing contact with your true nature. A sense of great betrayal arises, not just because your parents didn't see your real nature, but that you stopped seeing it...So because you are not in a state of total completeness, you feel guilty and bad, and have an attitude of punishing and hating yourself.[8]

---

8. Almaas, *Facets of Unity*, 95.

This is a particularly important point of realization for The Conquistador. When you lost basic trust in your early nurturing environment you split into two parts—your true self and your ego—and your ego took domain over your life. The ego creates conflict and opposition and welcomes the use of force to resolve life's challenges. Your true self knows your ego is an imposter but has little power to combat its authority without your intervention. This breach from divine power has generated feelings of sinfulness, badness, and overall guilt, to which you react with anger, spite, and vengeance. You become a fighter and not a lover. When you are successful in reestablishing your connection with your true self, you are, in effect, reestablishing connection with the divine energy field as well. Your ego has run wild and you have paid a very high price by striving to satisfy its needs no matter the cost. Now it is time to reposition your life so that struggling and fighting ceases; it was only necessary because you made the decision that it was. Go into the world knowing that it can be a kinder and gentler place than you ever thought possible.

#9: The Inner Nature of Everything Is Love

I have saved this Happiness Realization for last because it underpins all of the other realizations. The energy of the universe is fundamentally good, benevolent, and loving. It is interesting that nature does not contradict this assertion. The physicist Fred Alan Wolf offers the provocative assertion that light is love.

Many physicists believe that all matter is ultimately composed of trapped light...Hate, for example, is explained as a quantum statistical property of electrons—and no two electrons will ever exist in the same quantum state. While love, on the other hand, is explained in terms of quantum statistical behavior of photons—and all photons tend to move into the same state if given the chance. Thus, in a physical sense, the phrase 'light is love' is more than a metaphor.[9]

Wolf's description reminds me of John 8:12, "I am the light of the world." Light has always been associated with knowledge and love, as evidenced in the following phrases: "I saw the light"; "I became illuminated"; "Enlighten me"; "I feel the light of love"; "From darkness into the light"; "I just had a flash"; and "She is brilliant."

"That basis for spiritual power...has been developed...in regard to things unheard before, there arose in me vision, knowledge, wisdom, true knowledge and light."

—Buddha, *The Connected Discourses (Volume II)*

Few people are aware that human beings emit tiny elements of light. The German physicist, Fritz-Albert Popp, proved that small bits of light are stored and emitted from the DNA of our cells. His research also revealed that credible healers had stronger and

---

9. Wolf, *Mind Into Matter*, 46.

more vibrant light waves flowing from their hands than the average person. This lends additional credence to the notion that "light is love."

The ego is the opposite of love. It represents the darkness of the soul. The ego wants to know, "What's in it for me?" The ego's favorite words are "I" and "mine," and it does not give up without a fight. Believe it or not, the ego would rather cause your death than give up its power. Divine energy has the power to dissolve the ego and does not seek to possess but to transform darkness into light.

One of the most potent examples of divine love is a baby. Babies exist in a very strong attractor field of divine energy. Have you ever taken a baby to the mall and been walking along and pushing a stroller, and have total strangers come up to you and want to touch your baby? They are drawn into a very potent energy field of innocence and love. Yes, babies and puppies do something to us and it is not just because they are cute. They emit a radiance of something that we have lost: unobstructed and pure divine love.

Do you also notice that when those very same babies grow up into teenagers, no one would think of stopping their parents in the mall unless they planned to hit them over the head and rob them? Why is that? Though they are the same people, only older, something has weakened their energy field. Many teenagers have lost their faith and trust in life and have subsequently empowered their egos. Because of this, they no longer project this powerful attractor field because they have lost contact with it.

When you encounter divine energy it feels delightful, uplifting, and bright, as though the sun were shining with no clouds in the sky. True reality always has a quality of goodness about it, an expression of its deepest nature. It is impossible to remove love from divine energy and this energy field is inherent in everything in the world. Were you to encounter it without your conscious filters in place, you would be overwhelmed by the complete and total effusion of love that would course through every cell in your body. It would be like having a full body X-ray of divine love.

This Happiness Realization is particularly important for The Harmonizer, because you believe that love is conditional. During your early childhood you felt ignored or overlooked. You made the fateful observation that you were not lovable, that you were inferior in some way, that you did not deserve the attention you craved. From this you concluded that if you were more lovable you would command the attention you needed. These beliefs were pervasive and altered your life decisions. You carry the belief that if people really got to know you they would find you lacking and inferior. This deficiency has caused feelings of worthlessness and low self-esteem, of just not being good enough to get what you want out of life, of needing to settle for less because you don't have what it takes to rise to the occasion. Over time this has weakened and eroded your soul, a diminishment of your very being. You don't feel as though you deserve love, and have resigned yourself to the backwoods of happiness, and left yourself feeling lacking and fearful. When your ego is in charge and something goes wrong, you immediately conclude that it happened because you are deficient and inferior. Of course, this is a delusion that you have completely adopted as truth. You have suffered more than most from diminished opportunities and feelings of being a second-class citizen.

The truth is that you have not seen what is real. If you knew the truth you would recognize that you are beautiful, radiant, lovable, and full of value, and you would skip through the world with absolute confidence. In order to do this, you must wake up to your errors in judgment and recognize the limitations they have placed upon your life. This will not be an easy task for you. If you fail to take action, you are rejecting the golden light of divine energy that is in you and everything in your world. For you to accept your supposed flaws and limitations, you must hold a fundamental belief that the power of divine love does not exist in you or the world. You are not separate from the divine energy field, but, on the contrary, are a direct expression of it, including divine love. Nothing has the power to diminish you or remove your unique

> "The old adage 'you are what you eat' has changed into 'you are what you know' and since your knowledge ultimately depends on what information you accept as 'fact,' you are what you believe!"
>
> —Fred Alan Wolf, PhD, *Mind Into Matter: A New Alchemy of Science and Spirit*

expression of love to the world without you capitulating to your ego and letting it rampage through your life.

Thinking a Life

If we were to take one atom from my body and one atom from your body, they would be identical in every way. On the molecular level of nature the only difference between us is in form, not in substance. If you look deeper you see that atoms are composed primarily of open space. There really is very little there. What gives us our physical appearance is the speed of the electrons rapidly spinning around the nucleus of the atoms at close to the speed of light. If it were possible to stop these electrons from circling, we would disappear from the face of the earth. Our physical appearance is an illusion—a cosmic deception. We are nothing but open space. If we are not our bodies, what are we?

The evidence suggests that we are conscious awareness embedded in a world of our own creation. The world we experience is thought into existence and functions according to the rules we believe are at play. Every person on earth creates his own world based on what he accepts as truth. The world we all live in is malleable; it has no structure other than our notions about it. These beliefs become so deeply rooted within us that we are willing to base our life on them, and suffer and die for them even when there is absolutely no evidence of their truthfulness. We can't even recall when we accepted the truths we live by, who gave them to us, and certainly not their integrity. The ego believes that "the truth is what I say it is."

If we have the power to create our own world, it would be helpful to ground it in life-giving truth. In fact, our happiness depends upon it. I don't know about you but it is comforting to think that there is love in the world, that infinite intelligence is being expressed at every moment, and that I can relax because everything is not up to me. I like that; it is uplifting. And if a deeply cherished belief exists in your life that is hurting you, you can be assured that it is not an expression of divine spirit. Any belief that you have about yourself that limits or hurts you is false. That belief will lead you toward pain and destroy your happiness.

As human beings we have the power to change, but often not the will. Change comes from insight, a sudden realization that something is true. When this occurs, it either displaces our outmoded beliefs or modifies the beliefs that we already hold. Insights can either be major blockbusters that change our entire way of thinking or minor modifications that simply refine and amplify what we already believe to be true. Either way, they are precious commodities that are essential to our evolution and happiness.

By replacing falsehood with truth, we become more grounded in our living, more balanced in our thinking, and, most importantly, more aligned with the flow of divine energy. We exist in an interconnected universe that is constantly emitting the truth, even though we often have difficulty fully realizing it. When we encounter the truth it feels real and we are touched by it. The nine Happiness Realizations are an introduction to this truth; a shove off the dock so that you can travel down your own stream of self-realization.

If you would like to follow my regimen as you prepare for or adjust to retirement, review these nine Happiness Realizations every day for two to three minutes. Pay particular attention to the realization that addresses your specific E-Type. Create a list of the nine Happiness Realizations and attach it to your refrigerator, telephone, calendar, or computer monitor and read it every day for one year. Never skip a day. Take the list with you on vacation. It does not matter if you believe in the truthfulness of the realizations or not. It is not your job to do anything but let divine energy through the gateway of your consciousness. That is the only catalyst that is required for divine energy to begin doing its work of transformation. When I followed this routine for a period of months, I began to notice positive changes. The stress I had been feeling began to abate. I began to feel a greater sense of happiness. From personal experience, I have confidence in these realizations and strongly recommend them as a source of comfort as you traverse the retirement chasm.

Chapter 5

Living the Good Life

So far you have learned about the problem of achievement addiction, reviewed a description of your personality type, identified what types of activities offer you the highest potential for enjoyment, discovered beliefs and tendencies that may cause you unhappiness, and learned a set of realizations that have the power to uplift your spirit and bring more comfort and relaxation into your life. Hopefully you now possess greater insight and understanding to help guide you toward living the good life, but what is that exactly? This is an important question because every person planning his or her retirement eagerly anticipates "living the good life." There are some questions, however, regarding exactly what is required to achieve this goal. Contrary to many perceptions about retirement, I believe a successful transition into retirement means increasing your authenticity as a human being—turning up the wattage of your luminescence and letting the purity of your soul shine forth. This book isn't about helping you with your finances or providing you with tips on how to maintain your health. Instead, it is about helping you manage your psychological transition to retirement, which means increasing your happiness potential during the remaining years of your life. It is now time for your liberation. Listen to the church bells calling your name—all you need to do is answer, "I am coming." You are about to learn what it really means to live the good life.

It has been a long and hard road to get to this point in your life. As my father used to say, "If you live long enough, you'll see everything." But you have made it to an important inflection point. You are at a life intersection where you need to be introspective and make some important decisions, not only about the activities you would like to pursue, but how you want to "be" while you are pursuing them. Let's learn some new ways of being that are closer to your heart, embellish your soul, and bring out the best that is in you.

Let's Fall in Love

The love I am referring to is the love of life. Many of us fall out of love as we grow older; we lose our hold on it and let it slip through our fingers. We get worn down while just trying to cope with the challenges of living. We lose touch with the magic that we felt as children watching the rain fall, smelling the fall air, or rolling in freshly fallen snow. Do you remember? We thought anything was possible—that magic could happen at any moment. Sometimes my childhood memories are triggered by the scent of freshly cut grass or bread in the oven. The smells generate a warm feeling and I fondly recall happy times spent with my parents. How did we let these types of moments slip away?

I can recall the day I turned my back on love; it was the day I decided that money was the most important thing in my life. I had come to the conclusion that I had to redirect my career and dedicate myself to earning a good living. I didn't want to make a decent living—I wanted to make a lot of money. I wanted to be a success and live on the fast track. I felt that by attaining this goal I would live a more interesting and exciting life, provide greater security and opportunities for my children, and care for my parents in their old age. The day I decided to pursue this goal I weakened my connection to the divine energy field. I could feel its departure as it occurred, but didn't understand what was happening at the time.

On that day I left my position as a twelfth grade English teacher—where I pursued my passion for reading, literature, writing, and helping young people learn—and took a job in industry. I never gave it a second thought because I felt that I had to make it on my own, that success came from singleness of purpose, sacrifice, and staying on the straight and narrow. And even though I succeeded and gained pleasure from providing for my family, when I look back I realize that I disconnected from something important that was in me—I lost some special feelings of meaning and joy. It is difficult to visualize what my life would be like today if I had never made the decision to leave teaching. I missed interactions with students and my time in the school environment for a decade after I left.

I realize now that living in concordance with divine spirit fills you with energy; you do not need to supply it all by yourself. Living out of sync with it requires you to provide it all on your own and over time you become worn down and depleted. I believe that this is why some great musicians, singers, and writers work tirelessly into their later years and still feel energized by their work, and why those more disconnected from their inner source of joy count the days until they retire. You might say that God is where the love is.

Did you turn your back on love? Look back on your life. Is there something you need to reconnect with that gave you special delight and satisfaction when you were younger? Your old passion may be lying in a dormant state waiting for you to reignite it. You will reunite with old familiar feelings of joy and happiness when you recommence doing that important activity. One of the greatest benefits of retirement is having the time to pursue those things in life that bring you joy.

Blues Right Down to Your Soul

Many recent retirees may feel down or depressed as they confront their retirement and think of all the things they've lost or left behind. You can't get your life in the groove if you've got the blues. Great blues songs always tell the story of a painful personal loss with its accompanying mental anguish. The losses these sing-ers lament are not small or inconsequential, but are instead the kind that punch you in the gut—*Sugar, please don't leave me.* They are monumentally sorrowful and searing and can last a lifetime, leaving emotional scars. It could be the loss of your first love, your spouse, or girl- or boyfriend. It could even be the abrupt loss of a treasured job which slams you unexpectedly into retirement. These losses are often interpreted as self-esteem killers because they elicit feelings of doubt. You may think, *If only I were smarter/richer/handsomer/ prettier/thinner/sexier/more popular he or she would not leave me but love me.*

One of my all time favorite blues songs is, "I Can't Make You Love Me." According to Songfacts.com, the songwriting team of Mike Reid and Allen Shamblin wrote the song after reading a newspaper article about a man who shot at his girlfriend's car while drunk. "When the judge sentenced him and asked him what he had learned, he said, 'You can't make a woman love you if she don't.'"[1]

Bonnie Raitt, who popularized this song, reports that she felt such a wellspring of emotion while recording it, she was unable to sing it more than once. Later, she said during an interview with KGSR radio in Austin, Texas, that it was so sad a song, she couldn't recapture its emotion: "We'd try to do it again and I just said, 'You know, this ain't going to happen.'"[2]

---

1. "I Can't Make You Love Me by Bonnie Raitt," Songfacts.com, http://www.songfacts.com/detail.php?id=415.

2. Swapmeet Louie, "Bonnie Raitt: I Can't Make You Love Me," Frontloader.com, November 30, 2008, http://www.thefrontloader.com/2008/11/30/bonnie-raitt-i-cant-make-you-love-me/.

What makes the song's lyrics so emotional is the sense of sad resignation and powerlessness they evoke. There is the suggestion that you can't get what you want and need out of life because you lack the personal power to do so; you can't make people have feelings they don't.

Love is not something you can command; you can only encourage it to occur. Whether love comes or goes is not a judgment upon your worth as a human being, but is simply the unfolding of divine intelligence. There is no personal diminishment that occurs when loves does not come your way. The anguish felt from the blues—the sense that you cannot command the other person to do what you want—comes from the ego. If you hold the belief that life is revealing itself in accordance with a divine plan and have trust in its moment-to-moment revelations, you will not suffer the agony of the blues. The truth of the matter is that whatever brings you closer to divine energy works in your best interest in the long run; whatever separates you from divine energy weakens you. If a person is not capable of loving you it means that you are moving closer to truth and away from falsehood.

If you are harboring the blues, whether it be from a painful event that occurred forty years ago or yesterday, you have created an obstacle with the power to block you from living the good life during your retirement. Let your blues go with the full knowledge that the light of love is within you; you do not have to earn it, only recognize the essential truth of it.

Get on the Soul Train

The "soul train" leaves the station when you are approximately fifty years of age and arrives at its destination when you are around seventy-five. The sociologist Sara Lawrence-Lightfoot calls this period the "Last Chapter." This is an underground voyage that starts at the station called "Personality" and ends at the last stop—"Soul." Everyone boards this train, but most passengers get off before the scheduled destination.

The momentum of the soul train ride varies for each person. How fast we go depends mostly upon our level of awareness and the strength of our intention to arrive at our destination. Every once in a while, during our quiet moments, we can hear the whistle blow as a reminder that the train is at the station and calling us to get on board. Our car on this train is reserved just for us—it's private and exclusive—and no one can go in our place. Once on board it feels as though the train is powered by shimmering light, inexorably moving upward while being pulled by some powerful force that does not observe the natural laws of physics. This is a different place and one full of surprises.

Of course, our train is a metaphor for our evolution from personality to soul; moving from something man-made to something divine.

> "You don't have a soul. You are a soul. You have a body."
> —C. S. Lewis

Greater authenticity is the goal, the driving force behind our intentions. When we are authentic, we orbit the soul and feel its energy—we are the real deal. When we live in personality, we orbit around the ego and find ourselves in a painful prison of our own making.

We constructed our personality in order to navigate through the world we first encountered in our early childhood. It has helped and protected us through all the years, but it does not lead us home. The soul, on the other hand, is eternal and is what accompanies us when our time here is through. The personality is our shield; the soul is our true identity. Most people on earth want to progress toward the light, want access to inner truth, and know that their current life feels artificial compared to what it could be or was long ago. We are being pulled toward our authentic and real self as we become more self-aware.

It is very difficult to be consistently happy when we are living with a personality devoid of divine spirit because of the ephemeral nature of the ego. Rather than seeing things from an eternal perspective, the ego sees things from an hourly perspective—it believes in survival of the fittest. The ego is not compassionate. It is easily threatened because it knows it lacks legitimacy. It was created by man, not by God.

Living the good life requires you to get on the train and arrive at its ultimate destination. It means moving toward authenticity and away from ego. There is no trip more worth taking. When you exist in a state of authenticity, you are powerfully connected to life and naturally tend to do things for the benefit of others, rather than just for yourself. You possess soft power based on the rightness of being, rather than hard power based on force. You live in partnership with the divine energy field and are propelled by its intelligence and energy. Life is no longer a struggle; it is more yielding. You no longer need things; you need substance.

Play That Funky Music

Why is music so powerful? It's just auditory vibrations oscillating as waves of sound energy. The toughest person on earth can be touched by a song or uplifted by a melody. It is one of the great mysteries of life. There is a poignant moment in the movie *Copying Beethoven* when the actor Ed Harris, who plays Beethoven, makes the passionate statement:

> The vibrations on the air are the breath of God speaking to man's soul. Music is the language of God. We musicians are as close to God as man can be. We hear his voice, we read his lips, we give birth to the children of God, who sing his praise. That's what musicians are.[3]

When listening to music, the energy of our soul becomes entrained with the beat of the music and resonates with the sound's pulsations and tonal variations. It feels as if the music is coming from both inside as well as outside of us. Music completely bypasses the filter of our personality and entirely envelops our soul. This process is extremely powerful.

---

3. "Vibrations on the Air," *Copying Beethoven*, DVD, directed by Agnieszka Holland (Century City, CA: MGM Studios, 2006).

One woman, Bonnie, described an experience she had with a Toltec shaman by the name of Koyote. She relates what happened while she was participating in a drumming circle and listening to tribal music combined with a story: "After a short time there was something very magical happening in the space... We lost consciousness of our egos and became one with the storyteller."[4] Music expands our grandness of being, warms our soul, brings back memories and promotes our health. Music is like food for the soul, it feeds us something we cannot get anywhere else.

There are several types of sounds that may be interpreted as music, such as the ringing of church bells, the meowing of a cat, the whistling of a train, the barking of a dog, the chirping of birds, the roaring of a car engine, and the cheering of a crowd at a sporting event. We each interpret different sounds as music—it's a personal and intimate choice. Because of the unparalleled power of music, we need to make sure that we integrate our own unique brand of sound into our lives as much as possible.

When music pleases us, it is not our personality that feels the music, but our soul. I once heard someone comment that the voice of Andrea Bocelli was like hearing God sing. That statement may not be far from the truth. My mother could not listen to his music without crying.

---

4. Bonnie (artistpriestess), comment on "Shamanism and Drumming," World Tree, comment posted August 30, 2007, http://worldtree.tribe.net/thread/544b3090-2eb6-42d4-b8af-f8e0e4d0044b#d3b3c2ef-603f-4ab1-8c62-005d5b63bce1.

Be conscious of the music around you and never underestimate its power to elevate your being and bring you into closer contact with your soul. I discovered that retirement is often accompanied by emotional stresses and strains that seem to arise from some mysterious place for an obscure reason. Music goes directly to the source of that anxiety and offers a soothing balm to the troubled heart.

The Power of Place

It has been said that there are only three important decisions you make in life: what you do, whom you do it with, and where you do it. Often, where we do it is not our choice but a decision made for us by our jobs or life events. In our modern society, we must be flexible and move to where economic opportunities can be found. Our lives can get shuffled and we may land somewhere without planning or forethought.

I have learned that there is something called "the power of place." By this I mean that there are some geographic locations that resonate positively with us and others that don't. For example, twelve years ago I moved only forty minutes from my home in Princeton, New Jersey, to a rural area in Pennsylvania. To me it was like moving to a different country. I found myself happier and more comfortable in my new surroundings. It just fit. This positive energy continues to this day, with no diminishment over the years. My place in Pennsylvania feels like home, whereas my New Jersey location, which was quite beautiful, never provided me with a sense of comfort or belonging. Over the years, I have spoken with friends and acquaintances that have experienced similar reactions to places in their own lives.

Some retirees who have moved to the Sunbelt—a popular region to retire to—report feeling disjointed after their relocation. They indicate that they could never get used to their new environment. Recent studies have shown that combining the major stresses related to retirement, along with a relocation to a new state, can cause some people overwhelming anxiety because of the immensity of the change that occurs all at once. Some end up moving back to their old cities and towns. A *USA Today* article titled, "Older Seniors Return North," describes the growing trend of "boomerang" retirees, those retirees who return to pre-retirement homes to be near their children. [5] Charles Longino, director of the gerontology program at Wake Forest University, calls them "assistance migrants" because they return home needing living assistance from family members and their community.

I was born and raised in a small town southwest of Pittsburgh, Pennsylvania. I am continually amazed at the feelings of loyalty expressed by the people who have left this area and relocated around the country, mostly for greater economic opportunity. There is something called the Steeler Nation, which is akin to a sweeping cultural movement. You can go to almost any city in

5. Haya El Nasser, "Older Seniors Return North," *USA Today,* February 22, 2007, http://www.usatoday.com/news/nation/2007-02-21-aging-seniors_x.htm.

the country and find a sports bar showing Pittsburgh Steelers football games on game day. There is nothing like it. I, and hundreds of thousands of Pittsburgh expatriates, feel close to home when watching these games, and when seeing the skyline and Three Rivers Stadium. This is the power of place.

Your comfort with your immediate surroundings is a very individual decision. Many people can live anywhere and be happy; others need a certain type of energy that can only be provided by specific locals. For example, people who live in and around New York City and become accustomed to the city's fast pace, theatre, shopping, and museums, often find it difficult to find another equally satisfying area. I have also encountered people living in California who relish the laid-back culture, the moderate temperatures, the beach, and the overall lifestyle. They often find it difficult to replicate this environment in any other location.

If you are "location sensitive," it means that you need to live in an area that is on the same frequency as you. This is a personal decision, but you will know it when you feel it. Different cities, towns, and rural areas emit a very distinct type of energy, some compatible with you and some not. I believe living the good life includes being in tune with your environment and feeling inspired by its nature, views, climate, architecture, people, culture, and overall energy. If you can discover your special place in the world it will enhance your happiness and overall satisfaction. Location is an important component to living the good life and will contribute greatly to your life in retirement.

Being of Service

There are very few things in life that offer as many positive qualities as giving. Being of service is not an action but a life orientation—a way of positioning yourself within the divine energy field. Being of service is not about how good it makes you feel, how it embellishes your ego, or how it elevates your self-esteem; it is more an act of giving reciprocal energy to the divine energy field. When you provide a service to someone you give to everyone, including yourself. There is an energy transmission that occurs between the giver and the receiver: feelings of gratitude, appreciation, and thankfulness. These positive energy streams move both ways—to the receivers and back to the givers.

A few years ago a friend of mine wanted to help me with a task. I thought it was too difficult and required too much effort on his part, and so I politely refused, indicating that I could not possibly accept the act of friendship that was being offered. I will never forget his response, "Please don't refuse me this blessing." I was completely taken aback. He considered it a blessing to help me and asked me to accept his offer, not for my sake but for his own. How could I refuse?

Being of service creates light and energizes the divine energy field within you. It resembles a celestial tango of positive energy that cascades forward into all involved. You have heard people described as "doing God's work." This is accurate terminology. People who have mastered the art of giving find themselves living within the flow of divine energy. They can feel the positive energy—they are touched by the acts of compassion and kindness that they transmit to others. This energy is not originating from their personalities but from the divinity within them—their essence. We are made for this work; it is not a foreign act that occurs outside the realm of humanity. Every act of service we perform that is not in dedication to our ego is an action taken by our soul—by divine truth.

Many acts of service reduce the suffering in others. Buddha lived three thousand years ago and espoused much wisdom regarding the causes of suffering. He believed that everyone suffers from birth, sickness, old age, and death. We also suffer from being with those we dislike, being apart from those we love, and not getting what we want. The Buddha did not deny that there is happiness in life, but he pointed out that it does not last forever. Eventually everyone meets with some kind of suffering. He said: "There is happiness in life, happiness in friendship, happiness of a family, happiness in a healthy body and mind...but when one loses them, there is suffering."

It is difficult to conceive of happiness without showing compassion and service to others. We have all heard about the benefits associated with committing small random acts of kindness, a sort of astral chain letter. There is transformative power present at each moment during acts of giving, service, and compassion. When you retire, search out opportunities for service, and stay aware of the status of friends and neighbors. You will enrich your life and the lives of those around you through your helpfulness and kindness. That is an essential aspect of living the good life.

Yielding to the Wind

There are fundamental life lessons associated with tai chi, the martial art form that values slow movements meant to expand the mind and focus the body's energy. Many of tai chi's movements result from close observations of nature. There is a well-known story about Chang San-feng, who witnessed a fight between a bird and a snake, and observed how the soft and yielding could overcome the hard and inflexible. Lao-tzu described the power of yielding in several numbered poems. In chapter 22 of the *Tao te Ching*, he wrote, "Yield and overcome; Bend and be straight."[6]

Lao-tzu exhorts his followers to be like water, which flows humbly along, yet has the capability of wearing away the hardest of stone. He uses this as a metaphor to illustrate that the weak and flexible can overcome the strong and rigid through the subtle use of natural intrinsic force.

The principles of yielding, softness, centeredness, slowness, balance, suppleness, and rootedness are all elements of tai chi. It is all about yielding to the opponent with the idea of using flexibility as an offensive strategy. Of course this requires a great deal of mental as well as physical training. However, there is no doubt that tai chi masters can do amazing things while

---

6. Bjørn Darboe Nissen, "Tai Chi and Taoism," Tai Chi Philosophy, http://www.chi.dk/tai_chi_philosophy.htm.

appearing totally relaxed. It is as if they have learned to defy the natural laws of physics. This, of course, is not the case. They have learned a deeper truth about the hidden reality of nature.

Why is yielding so important to living the good life? As you enter retirement you will encounter headwinds that may challenge your happiness, including such obstacles as death of a loved one, ill health, or financial losses. What will be your response? The best approach is to yield—bend with the wind—so that you may snap back when the crisis is over. As we learned from Lao-tzu, yielding is an act of strength, not of weakness. It is integration with the divine energy field that is supportive and uplifting.

There Is No Beginning—There Is No End

We have been taught that things are created and evolve in a discrete fashion; there is a beginning, middle, and end. Everything has its time and then moves on to extinction. We live a singular existence based on the cycle of life and the natural laws of birth and death. We can witness this sequence in our own lives and those of our loved ones; it is irrefutable. When we were born, that was the beginning; when we die, that will be the end.

If we restrict our thinking to the linear world of things, there is clear evidence that this line of thought is true. Yes, everything is constantly changing, and this change is one of disintegration. Aging is a good example of deterioration over time—we don't need to be reminded of this fact. But what of the nonlinear world? Does it function according to the same evolutionary cycle?

A few years ago I had the good fortune to view the *Pietà*, a famous sculpture by Michelangelo, in Florence, Italy. The emotional effect the work had on me was so unexpected and intense that I had to take a seat in order to regain my composure. I felt energy radiate from the sculpture right into me. Did that experience have a beginning, middle, and end? Does inspiration dissipate over time? Will any of Michelangelo's sculptures ever stop expressing their beauty? Does our light go out when our time is through?

> "A man's true wealth is the good he does in the world. Beauty is eternity gazing at itself in a mirror. But you are eternity and you are the mirror."
>
> —Khalil Gibran

If we review the most revered religious traditions in the world, we discover that there is general agreement that our essence is eternal. The concurrence in every major spiritual tradition is that when our body dies, our soul remains as an eternally imprinted awareness that retains its own unique conscious energy. What is real and true in us lives on after our deaths. When our day is done, we reunite or reintegrate with divine energy.

I can recall one occasion when my father, sitting at the kitchen table, said to me, "You know Rob, I feel just the same inside as I always have."

"Dad, what are you talking about? You're ninety years old."

"I know that but I am talking about how I feel inside. I just don't feel old."

I later realized what he was trying to tell me. He wanted me to know that even though his body had aged, his spirit—his very soul—had not aged at all. It was as it always had been—eternal. It was a revelation to him and an important lesson for me.

This notion of the eternal existence of the human spirit is of the highest importance imaginable. If it is true, what are the implications for our life and how we live it? First of all, it appears that there are two forms of truth: surface truth and deep truth. Modern society operates off of a surface truth paradigm. Make money, be successful. Do whatever it takes and go to any extreme to be victorious, and always be aware that the bad guys are gaining on you. This life is not about meaning; it's about winning.

Deep truth lives on the ground floor of our existence. We have seldom lived within its influence because many of us have failed to consider or think deeply about the nonlinear field of consciousness that is uniquely ours, and travels through all of eternity, not just one lifetime. This is our very own uniquely imprinted energy field that links us to the prime source of all existence. Its language is truth in the absolute.

It is clear that there is an aspect of us that transcends time. Given this truth, it would be wise to live our lives as if our souls really matter. Doing what is best for our souls is the most important thing in life—it should transcend everything. When the curtain comes down and we are left standing, our soul is who and what we really are—it represents our eternal truth. Take good care of your soul because it is the only thing you have that will last forever.

Chapter 6

The Light of Life

So here we are. Shall we cross the great divide together? Of course you know by now that the divide is within each of us and nowhere else.

Matthew 19:24 states, "It is easier for a camel to go through the eye of a needle, than for a rich man to enter the kingdom of God." There are many interpretations of

> "Except ye become as little children, ye will not enter the kingdom of heaven."
>
> —Matthew 18:3

this well-known passage; I choose to believe it is about ego domination. In biblical terms, when you are labeled "rich" it means that you have subscribed to the laws of the linear domain to the exclusion of the divine energy field—you have worshipped at the altar of material goods. "Rich" means being anchored to the false world of the ego, while real wealth means living in accordance with the divine energy field and staking your life on its transcendence. If you cannot neutralize your ego, you will have difficulty aligning with the loving energy of the divine field.

> "I am the Light that is above them all, I am the All.
> The All came from me, and the All has returned to me.
> Split wood and I am there. Raise a stone and you will find me."
>
> —The Gospel of Thomas, verse 77

When we were children our egos had not gained preeminence in our lives; we lived in innocent accordance with the divine energy field. Little children trust in the natural flow. They are attuned to the magic of the ever-unfolding underlying forces of life and do not question their validity. They have intuitive insight and are anchored in the radiant field of divine spirit. Watch them closely. How do they behave? Are they suspicious, striving, callous, combative, grasping, desperate, or self-promoting? The answer is no. This biblical passage means that you cannot be at peace and project radiant light if you subscribe to the dictates of the ego. This is the great divide.

Happiness in your life means being real, authentic, and connected to divine ground. It requires removing all that is not genuine to reveal all that is beautiful and pristine. Divine ground is your base camp, a place where you are nurtured and gain strength. It is connected to an inexhaustible energy source that transcends the world as we know it.

The Enneagram is a small segment of this energy source, a peek into the truth. It represents a starting place that is outside the realm of convention. It discloses a special place within you that reveals who you are and what you need to do to polish your lantern and brighten your light.

Your happiness at this important juncture is a decision, a stated intention to grow into a new life called retirement. Entering this new stage of existence offers an exciting opportunity to expand your knowledge and reveal more of the special gifts that are within you. Retirement offers the freedom and opportunity to explore life's mysteries and make decisions that will transcend time. It may require courage on your part and a strong conviction to discard aspects of yourself that no longer serve your best interests. In order to achieve happiness in this new phase, you may need to become more attuned to your distinctive nature and reassess your spiritual convictions. So be it. There is no better time to embark on this journey than this very moment. There is a part of you that knows this—understands the rules of this game. You would not be reading this book to the very last page if something real in you had not surfaced—if the words in this book had not connected with the truth that is in you. Growth awaits you—change is afoot—your new life is waiting. It is time to go.

The E-Type Questionnaire

Directions: Read the following statements carefully and decide to what extent they accurately describe you. Write the number of your answer choice in the space marked "Score." It is very important to indicate how you see yourself at this moment, not how you once were or how you would like to be.

1. I enjoy solving difficult problems, even in my spare time.
(1) No, not at all
(2) No, not much
(3) Yes, sometimes
(4) Yes, definitely
Score _____

2. I have a romantic nature.
(1) No, not at all
(2) No, not much
(3) Yes, sometimes
(4) Yes, definitely
Score _____

3. I like to create the right image in order to succeed.
(1) No, not at all
(2) No, not much
(3) Yes, sometimes
(4) Yes, definitely
Score _____

4. I have a flair for the dramatic.
(1) No, not at all
(2) No, not much
(3) Yes, sometimes
(4) Yes, definitely
Score _____

5. I like to be alone most of the time.
(1) No, not at all
(2) No, not much
(3) Yes, sometimes
(4) Yes, definitely
Score _____

6. I am the cautious type and am conservative by
nature.
(1) No, not at all
(2) No, not much
(3) Yes, sometimes
(4) Yes, definitely
Score _____

7. I have a sunny personality and people like me because I am interesting.
   (1) No, not at all
   (2) No, not much
   (3) Yes, sometimes
   (4) Yes, definitely
   Score _____

8. I find it difficult being successful without power and control.
   (1) No, not at all
   (2) No, not much
   (3) Yes, sometimes
   (4) Yes, definitely
   Score _____

9. I tend to procrastinate.
   (1) No, not at all
   (2) No, not much
   (3) Yes, sometimes
   (4) Yes, definitely
   Score _____

10. In my spare time I like to fix things.
   (1) No, not at all
   (2) No, not much
   (3) Yes, sometimes
   (4) Yes, definitely
   Score _____

11. I feel disappointment when others do not meet my expectations.
(1) No, not at all
(2) No, not much
(3) Yes, sometimes
(4) Yes, definitely
Score _____

12. I feel comfortable being in charge.
(1) No, not at all
(2) No, not much
(3) Yes, sometimes
(4) Yes, definitely
Score _____

13. I have been accused of being temperamental.
(1) No, not at all
(2) No, not much
(3) Yes, sometimes
(4) Yes, definitely
Score _____

14. I like to dream up new ideas.
(1) No, not at all
(2) No, not much
(3) Yes, sometimes
(4) Yes, definitely
Score _____

15. I am good at identifying things that could go wrong.
(1) No, not at all
(2) No, not much

(3) Yes, sometimes
(4) Yes, definitely
Score _____

16. I like to plan fun-filled outings.
(1) No, not at all
(2) No, not much
(3) Yes, sometimes
(4) Yes, definitely
Score _____

17. Confrontations do not bother me.
(1) No, not at all
(2) No, not much
(3) Yes, sometimes
(4) Yes, definitely
Score _____

18. I have a hard time knowing what I want.
(1) No, not at all
(2) No, not much
(3) Yes, sometimes
(4) Yes, definitely
Score _____

19. Others do not do things as precisely as I do.
(1) No, not at all
(2) No, not much
(3) Yes, sometimes
(4) Yes, definitely
Score _____

20. It is a high priority for me to stay in close touch with friends and family.
(1) No, not at all
(2) No, not much
(3) Yes, sometimes
(4) Yes, definitely
Score _____

21. I enjoy being the center of attention.
(1) No, not at all
(2) No, not much
(3) Yes, sometimes
(4) Yes, definitely
Score _____

22. I feel sad and melancholy a lot of the time.
(1) No, not at all
(2) No, not much
(3) Yes, sometimes
(4) Yes, definitely
Score _____

23. I like to do in-depth research in subjects that interest me.
(1) No, not at all
(2) No, not much
(3) Yes, sometimes
(4) Yes, definitely
Score _____

24. I am not much of a risk taker and like to plan carefully.
(1) No, not at all
(2) No, not much
(3) Yes, sometimes
(4) Yes, definitely
Score _____

25. I seldom feel depressed because there are so many interesting things to do.
(1) No, not at all
(2) No, not much
(3) Yes, sometimes
(4) Yes, definitely
Score _____

26. I charge forward even if I don't know the outcome.
(1) No, not at all
(2) No, not much
(3) Yes, sometimes
(4) Yes, definitely
Score _____

27. I have difficulty making decisions because I see all sides of an issue.
(1) No, not at all
(2) No, not much
(3) Yes, sometimes
(4) Yes, definitely
Score _____

28. I have a tendency to be too self-critical and demanding.
(1) No, not at all
(2) No, not much
(3) Yes, sometimes
(4) Yes, definitely
Score _____

29. I love taking care of children.
(1) No, not at all
(2) No, not much
(3) Yes, sometimes
(4) Yes, definitely
Score _____

30. Being successful is an essential part of my identity.
(1) No, not at all
(2) No, not much
(3) Yes, sometimes
(4) Yes, definitely
Score _____

31. I have a heightened sensitivity to others' emotions.
(1) No, not at all
(2) No, not much
(3) Yes, sometimes
(4) Yes, definitely
Score _____

32. I like exploring new ideas that others may feel
are "far-out."
(1) No, not at all
(2) No, not much
(3) Yes, sometimes
(4) Yes, definitely
Score _____

33. I have a hidden rebellious streak that often goes
unnoticed.
(1) No, not at all
(2) No, not much
(3) Yes, sometimes
(4) Yes, definitely
Score _____

34. Having excitement in my life is really important
to me.
(1) No, not at all
(2) No, not much
(3) Yes, sometimes
(4) Yes, definitely
Score _____

35. Competition brings out the best in me.
(1) No, not at all
(2) No, not much
(3) Yes, sometimes
(4) Yes, definitely
Score _____

36. It is hard for me to say "no."
(1) No, not at all
(2) No, not much
(3) Yes, sometimes
(4) Yes, definitely
Score _____

37. If I don't do it right, I don't do it at all.
(1) No, not at all
(2) No, not much
(3) Yes, sometimes
(4) Yes, definitely
Score _____

38. I am a loving person but have a stubborn streak.
(1) No, not at all
(2) No, not much
(3) Yes, sometimes
(4) Yes, definitely
Score _____

39. I can adapt myself to fit into almost any situation.
(1) No, not at all
(2) No, not much
(3) Yes, sometimes
(4) Yes, definitely
Score _____

40. If I could be anything, I would like to be a successful and passionate artist.
(1) No, not at all
(2) No, not much
(3) Yes, sometimes
(4) Yes, definitely
Score _____

41. I am uncomfortable at most social gatherings.
(1) No, not at all
(2) No, not often
(3) Yes, sometimes
(4) Yes, definitely
Score _____

42. If I like my boss I am a loyal employee.
(1) No, not at all
(2) No, not much
(3) Yes, sometimes
(4) Yes, definitely
Score _____

43. I get easily bored and am attracted to novelty and new experiences.
(1) No, not at all
(2) No, not much
(3) Yes, sometimes
(4) Yes, definitely
Score _____

44. I can intimidate others with my forcefulness.
(1) No, not at all
(2) No, not much
(3) Yes, sometimes
(4) Yes, definitely
Score _____

45. I avoid conflict whenever possible because it makes me uncomfortable.
(1) No, not at all
(2) No, not much
(3) Yes, sometimes
(4) Yes, definitely
Score _____

Answer Key

E-1	Score	E-2	Score	E-3	Score	E-4	Score	E-5	Score	E-6	Score	E-7	Score	E-8	Score	E-9	Score
Q1		Q2		Q3		Q4		Q5		Q6		Q7		Q8		Q9	
10		11		12		13		14		15		16		17		18	
19		20		21		22		23		24		25		26		27	
28		29		30		31		32		33		34		35		36	
37		38		39		40		41		42		43		44		45	
Total		Total		Total		Total		Total		Total		Total		Total		Total	

Using the Answer Key above, enter your answer score (1–4) in the score column next to each question. For example, if your score for question 1 were 2, then you would enter a 2 in the score column next to Q1. If your score for question 10 were 3, then you would enter a 3 in the score column next to Q10. After entering all of your answers in the appropriate columns, total each one. Your totals from each column represent your score for each of the nine E-Types.

What is your highest score? If you have a total E-Type score from 18–20, there is a strong possibility that you have identified your correct type. If you have a score from 16–17 there is some possibility that this is your type.

It is not always easy to identify your correct type. Occasionally, it takes some additional deliberation and self-discovery. If you continue to lack confidence in the identification of your E-Type, you may benefit from reading one or more of the books listed in Recommended Reading.

Recommended Reading

For those interested in learning more about the Enneagram, here are some classic introductory texts you may find helpful and interesting.

Daniels, David, and Virginia A. Price. *The Essential Enneagram*. New York: HarperCollins, 2009.

Palmer, Helen. *The Enneagram in Love and Work*. New York: HarperCollins, 1995.

Riso, Don Richard. *Discovering Your Personality Type*. New York: Houghton Mifflin Company, 2003.

———. *Personality Types*. New York: Houghton Mifflin Company, 1996.

———. *Understanding the Enneagram*. New York: Houghton Mifflin Company, 2000.

Riso, Don Richard and Russ Hudson. *The Wisdom of the Enneagram*. New York: Bantam Books, 1999.

Bibliography

Almaas, A. H. *Diamond Heart, Book One: Elements of the Real in Man.* Boston: Shambhala, 2000.

———. *Facets of Unity: The Enneagram of Holy Ideas.* Berkley, CA: Diamond Books, 1998.

Bodhi, Bhikkhu. *The Connected Discourses of the Buddha: A New Translation of the Samyutta Kikaya.* Somerville, MA: Wisdom Publications, 2000.

Braden, Gregg. *The Divine Matrix: Bridging Time, Space, Miracles, and Belief.* New York: Hay House, 2007.

Capra, Fritjof. *The Hidden Connections: Integrating the Biological, Cognitive, and Social Dimensions of Life into a Science of Sustainability.* New York: Doubleday, 2002.

Csikszentmihalyi, Mihaly. *Flow: The Psychology of Optimal Experience.* New York: Harper Perennial, 1990.

Dalai Lama. *How to Practice: The Way to a Meaningful Life.* Translated and edited by Jeffrey Hopkins. New York: Atria Books, 2002.

Deng, Ming-Dao. *Everyday Tao: Living with Balance and Harmony*. New York: HarperCollins, 1996.

Gladwell, Malcolm. *Outliers: The Story of Success*. New York: Little, Brown, 2008.

Hartmann, Thom. *The Last Hours of Ancient Sunlight: Waking Up to Personal and Global Transformation*. New York: Harmony Books, 1999.

———. *The Prophet's Way: Touching the Power of Life*. Northfield, VT: Mythical Books, 1997.

Hawkins, David R. *Power vs. Force: The Hidden Determinants of Human Behavior*. Carlsbad, CA: Hay House, 2002.

———. *Transcending the Levels of Consciousness*. Sedona, AZ: Veritas Publishing, 2006.

James, *William. The Varieties of Religious Experience*. 1902. Reprint, New York: Barnes & Noble, 2004.

Lao-tzu. *Tao te Ching*. Translated by Stephen Mitchell. New York: Harper & Row, 1988.

Lardani, Andrea and Raul Correa. "A Preventive Approach to Retirement." *Journal of Employee Assistance* (March 2005) http://findarticles.com/p/articles/mi_m0PLP/is_1_35/ai_n17208168/

Lawrence-Lightfoot, Sara. *The Third Chapter: Passion, Risk, and Adventure in the 25 Years after 50*. New York: Sarah Crichton Books, 2009.

McTaggart, Lynne. *The Field: The Quest for the Secret Force of the Universe*. New York: HarperCollins, 2002.

———. *The Intention Experiment: Using Your Thoughts*

to Change Your Life and the World. New York: Free Press, 2007.

Mindell, Arnold. *Quantum Mind: The Edge Between Physics and Psychology*. Portland, OR: Lao Tse Press, 2000.

Naranjo, Claudio. *Character and Neurosis: An Integrative View*. 1994, Nevada City, CA: Gateways/IDHHB, 1994.

Pink, Daniel H. *A Whole New Mind: Why Right-Brainers Will Rule the Future*. New York: The Penguin Group, 2006.

Pipher, Mary. *Another Country: Navigating the Emotional Terrain of our Elders*. New York: Riverhead Books, 1999.

Rivele, Stephen J. and Christopher Wilkinson. "Vibrations on the Air." *Copying Beethoven*. DVD. Directed by Agnieszka Holland. Century City, CA: MGM Studios, 2006.

Schlossberg, Nancy K. *Retire Smart, Retire Happy: Finding Your True Path in Life*. Washington, DC: American Psychological Association, 2004.

Stapp, Henry P. *Mindful Universe: Quantum Mechanics and the Participating Observer*. New York: Springer, 2007.

Walker, Evan Harris. *The Physics of Consciousness: The Quantum Mind and the Meaning of Life*. New York: Basic Books, 2000.

Wallace, B. Alan. *Choosing Reality: A Buddhist View of Physics and the Mind*. Ithaca, NY:, Snow Lion Publications, 1996.

Wei, Wu. *I Ching Wisdom: Guidance from the Book of Changes.* Los Angeles: Power Press, 1994.

Wilber, Ken, ed. *Quantum Questions: Mystical Writings of the World's Greatest Physicists.* Boston: Shambhala, 2001.

Wolf, Fred Alan. *Mind into Matter: A New Alchemy of Science and Spirit.* Portsmouth, NH: Moment Point Press, 2001.